X–MEDIUM

Ella Lehmus

X–MEDIUM

The way from darkness to light

Unfortunately, I cannot guarantee the complete accuracy of the text.

Typos and misunderstandings are possible.

However, this story is about my own life, and it is based on true events. Some names and descriptions of places have been changed.

ONE

Since I was a child, I had intuition about what was going to happened. My mother told me, that in the age of two I was telling in advance some things that were really happening. Sometimes those things were happening within few hours.

Once I have kept saying that my aunt will visit us with her daughter. We did not have a phone and neither any appointment for a visit has not been done. Funny, but I do remember that.

I was sitting on the bed, covered with a mustard-colored blank. I was wearing white pantyhose and a dress. I had to patter: – Anni and Minttu will visit us. Anni and Minttu will visit us.
I was continuing pattering of it, and I remember my mother was getting a bit annoyed because of that. In a while Anni and Minttu were behind our door. They were living 25 km away, so they have

been leaving their home already when I started pattering.

I remembered many things happening in my early years and my mother always kept saying it is impossible for me to remember. But I did and I do.

I was 12 months old when I got high fever. The thermometer was no longer enough, and father had called a doctor for us from the neighbor. I told my mother about that night decades later and she was amazed.

– It was raining, weather was awful. The rain was lashing the living room window hard, I started. I was lying on the brown fabric couch in the living room on top of a red blanket, facing the window. I did see the whole room at once, as if I was at the edge of the ceiling at the same time as I was lying on that sofa. Then father went to turn on the outside light and soon a man in a black robe entered the front door, I continued the story and mother listened more closely.

– The man was wearing a black hat and black raincoat, and he was carrying big black bag. He had a bland and silver colored stethoscope and it felt cold, I was remembering.

– No one has been ever telling you that, Ella, my mother said. – How an earth can you remember that? she was wondering.

– I don't know, I just remember clearly, I answered.

– The doctor indeed had a black hat and black raincoat, and it was raining like cats and dogs then, mother told and was still wondering. – And you had over 40 °C (104 °F) fever and you were convulsing.

When I was about 8 years old, I woke up in my room which was in the top floor of our house. I could not sleep after waking up and I went sneaking downstairs to my parents' bedroom. I wanted to ask if I could sleep with them for the rest of the night.

I descended the stairs and went to the hall.

The hallway led to the kitchen and from the kitchen to mom and dad's bedroom. I had a blue nightgown with yellow lion pictures on it. I stayed in the doorway between the hall and the kitchen, wondering if I was too old to ask to sleep with mom and dad. But at the same time, I saw myself at the door of the kitchen and the parents' bedroom, talking and complaining that I couldn't sleep. I looked at myself from five meters away and felt embarrassed. So, I was embarrassed by what I did there, when I had just thought about going. Part of me was standing at the other door and part of me was standing there at the parents' bedroom door. These events confused my family, but to me they were quite ordinary. Telling them later convinced certain groups that I had the skills of a seer.

I was 11 years old when my father got seriously ill. I was collecting leaves from the nature, crushed them and diluted in water. Then I poured the liquid to the blue glass bottle and saved in my room. I thought it will cure my father. I kept the bottle years after my father died, I kept it until all the liquid has been evaporated. I wanted to cure the cancer from the whole world one day.

On my father's last day, my whole family and I visited him, and he prayed the evening prayer for us. I was crying the whole time, and I couldn't understand what my father was saying, because the cancer had already ravaged his brain, and his words were slurred.

We returned home and I sat with my mother at the kitchen table. The table was placed in front of a large window. We looked out together as a huge swan flew with open wings towards the window behind which we were sitting. Both of us, mother and I, were speechless. Just before the swan would have hit the window it turned straight up. It was an amazing sight that we couldn't believe.
– Eero !! my mother called my father's name in a panic. I knew that father has went to the heaven. The mother suddenly got up from the chair and said she was going back to the hospital.

– I'm coming too, I said and got up as well.

– Ella, you are staying home, mother said in her determined tone, which I usually did not dare to question. – No, I want to come with you, I sobbed and cried.

– Ella, NO! The matter was not discussed further. My mother went to the neighbor and got a lift to the hospital.

Waiting at home was excruciating pain. I knew what had happened, but I refused to believe it. When the mother finally arrived back home, she said that the father was already dead when she got there. I fell to my knees and screamed out loud. I was completely broken. Why the God I prayed to every night had taken my father away. – Dad, come back, I was screaming and crying.

There was no end to the crying at all, in the end I was completely exhausted and shaking. I didn't want to sleep until dad came back. My mother was devastated, but she tried to comfort me. My other siblings were also grieving, but grief hit me the deepest.

I was in agony, and at that time there was no one to help to and talk about my feelings. Of course, there were psychiatrists in big cities, but we couldn't afford that, and psychiatric therapy was only given to crazy people, as they used to say in our small village. That day I cried out in grief and

kept asking my mother why God took my father
away.
– Why is God so cruel mother? I was yelling while
crying.
Mom had no answer, but she tried her best to
comfort me. I prayed to myself and out loud,
crying out to God to bring dad back. I don't
remember how I ended up sleeping, I apparently
cried myself to sleep on the kitchen floor and my
mother carried me into the sleeping room. That
night, all my siblings and mother, we slept in the
same room.
   I woke up to someone calling me.
– Ella, Ella, the voice said.
It was dad's voice! I was fully awake at once. I saw
a figure near my bed that smelled like my father,
whose contours also resembled him, and this
creature felt like my father. It WAS my father. My
mouth felt open as I gazed mesmerized at that
shimmering figure. Then I was overcome with
great fear. – But father is dead, I thought.
– Don't be afraid Ella, the voice of my father said.
That figure was close to me, and it resembled a
silver-colored sand, but its outline and everything
about it was like my father.
I quickly pulled the blanket over my head. I was
really scared. There, under the blanket, I started to
think that I shouldn't be afraid of dad. If God had
sent my father back. I lowered the blanket over my

head and looked for that figure with my eyes. I didn't see it again though. I started crying again. I blamed myself for scaring dad away.

In the morning I told my mother about what happened. Mom stroked my head and comforted me. However, she did not comment on what happened. For years after that, I always prayed the same prayer in the evenings. In that prayer, I asked my father to come back.
I knew it was impossible, but I prayed anyway, year after year.

Later, at the dawn of puberty, I left that part out of the prayer. There was no end to the sadness and pain, and that pain was repeated later every time I started dating.

I was so afraid of being left behind that I clung and always made that fear come true. I had a big wound of rejection. I mourned each broken relationship as if the world was ending and me with it.

I had already decided at the age of fifteen that I would not have children. I had also decided that it was best to be alone – no need to suffer. However, that solitude did not materialize; I met men and dated for short and slightly longer periods. Relationships ended to my own pain. Then, in my thirties, I decided that maybe it would really be best to be alone.

However, fate decided otherwise, and I met a very special man – Pekka.

Sometimes I thought that I would write a book about our six-year relationship, because a lot happened during those six years and that time had a profound effect on the rest of my life. Both the police and the women's shelter became familiar. It was also suggested to me to change my identity and move out of the town.

I have had many teachers in my life, but Pekka has been the best of them all.

It is said that a person learns from what he experiences and often the hard way. That's exactly what happened to me.

I also had a child with Pekka, as planned. That child was and still is the most precious thing in the world to me.

T W O

My relationship with Pekka had just ended and I was like a fragile shell. I was mentally and physically fragile, my clothes were hanging off me and I was malnourished.

I had to hide and secure my passage, plan every step. I was flashing behind me all the time and I couldn't relax; I was on alert all the time.

My friend Eva wanted to help me and told me about a woman who heals with energy. Eva had been under the care of this woman, and she said that woman knew things about her that no one else knew.

– The feeling was incredible after the therapy, Eva beamed.

– What kind of feeling? I asked.

– Light and happy. Ella, you absolutely must try it! I wouldn't have been able to handle anything, but Eva didn't give up.

– I'll make an appointment for you now, I have the number here, shall we call?
– No but give me the number and I'll call from home.
– Do you promise, Eva said. – I promise, I said, and we slapped our palms together. At home I pondered the matter in my mind and the voice of reason said:
– Don't believe all the hype.
However, the feeling was stronger, and it even urged me to come. What would I have to lose, life is in pieces, if I could breathe again after a long time. As the morning dawned, I picked up the phone and called to make an appointment.

   I went to Maiju's energy healing room early in the morning, sometime after a couple of weeks after Eva's persuasion. She told me on the phone there were no appointments earlier, there was a queue of customers.
– Well, hey Ella, said Maiju with a flattering smile on her face.
– It can't be true, I thought. – I know that Maiju. She is the same Maiju who bullied me as a child. She lied as much as he could and bombarded her younger ones. She made tricks and was mean. I should have been asking the whole name or before making appointment.
– Hello, I replied timidly.

I immediately wished I hadn't come, but it would be really embarrassing to leave. I'm always so kind and I do everything to please others, or I was!

Maiju was still smiling, or I think grinning is a more descriptive word for her expression. She asked me to lie on the therapy table. I settled into it as she instructed, and she put on soft music. That music sounded like the chanting of the Indians, and gentle drumming could be heard in the background.

Maiju said that my megahertz are high. I was laughed at. I've never been any good at physics, but I knew that much that megahertz can't be measured from humans.

– How so high? I asked, and when I asked, I realized that there was no need to ask. Maiju got upset and didn't answer. – Well, who has been taking your energies? Maiju was asking sarcastic in a while.

– Um, I don't know, I replied confused. Maybe my ex-husband, I continued.

I wouldn't have wanted to talk about my affairs, and at least not to her.

– Oh, why did I come, I should have found out who it was first, I thought.

However, I decided to try to relax. Maiju asked me a couple of different times to calm down and relax.

– Well, at least I'm safe from my ex-husband here, I thought, and my body slowly began to press

against the therapy table. For the rest of the time, Maiju was quiet and that felt good. I calmed down and I think I was on the verge of sleep. I hadn't slept very well in a long time since my ex-husband's threats, so the rest was good. At the end of the energy healing therapy, Maiju said she saw a lot of red energy and a man.
– What does it mean? I asked.
– Red is the color of hate energy.
– Oh yeah, I wondered and thought at the same time, how can Maiju know that.
– All this can be seen in your energy field, Ella, Maiju said.
I was confused and asked if she was reading my mind? – Ha ha, you could call it that, Maiju laughed.
   Maiju told me that I have many invisible helpers and guides.
– You have also been prayed for, she said quietly.
– This is it; this is exactly what I've been looking for, a big thought popped into my head. – We need to get more of this.
   At the end of the therapy, Maiju said that she would recommend me another time, but her calendar is very full.
– So many people go to this kind of healing therapy, I thought.

– At the end of the month, you might find an appointment, will you take it? Maiju asked, scrolling through her calendar.
– I'll take it, I said.
    On the way home I felt dizzy and felt a bit confused. It made me wonder how a bully had become a helper.
– She must have become religious or something, there were angels hanging here and there, I thought.
    My next energy healing appointment was in a month, and I was really looking forward to it. I left the healing room again, half dizzy. I had experienced wonderful energies and Maiju had seen them around me.

When the energy healing therapies had continued for about half a year, I felt that I had recovered nicely from being a victim of my ex-husband. However, it was also influenced by the peer support group I attended, and a new love had also entered the picture. However, in Maiju's opinion, that love had not helped me.
– It's such a patchwork relationship, she poked. I was a little hurt, and that left me wondering. I didn't really want to believe Maiju.
    I started to feel that I would no longer get a response from Maiju's energy healing therapy, and I thought of taking a break.

After one energy therapy session, I said that I
would not order another appointment now.
– I don't know if I can take you anymore, the times
are so reserved, Maiju said complainingly.
– Well, in that case, I'll make a new appointment
right away, I said.

The next appointment was found exactly one
month later.
    That next time was different.
– Tell me, Ella, what do you see? Maiju said
suddenly.
I had sunk into a wonderful state of relaxation, and
I was watching the wonderful blue color that
turned into shades of red and purple with my eyes
closed. I was startled and talked about these colors.
– Oooooh, exclaimed Maiju. – Exactly! Those are
the colors there, she continued excitedly.
– Oh yeah, I said. So, she saw the same thing as
me, pretty amazing! But a small flicker of doubt
would cross my mind.
– You could come and take care of this, we could
change places, Maiju continued convincingly.
– Well, I guess not, I said modestly.
– Yes, you ARE the helper, Maiju assured.
That was a nice touch to my often-battered self-
esteem.
– Wow, if only it were like that, oh If only it were,
I thought hopefully.

I continued with Maiju's energy healing therapies regularly about once a month. Maiju saw everything for me; she said she saw my spirit guides, power animals and past lives.
– You have been the pharaoh's wife, Maiju said once in the middle of the energy therapy.
– You have had mystical powers and you have also been worshipped, she continued.
– Oh, you are beautiful in this life, absolutely dazzling, Maiju exclaimed so that I was scared.
– Hey, don't be afraid, anything can happen during this therapy, Maiju laughed.
It didn't make me laugh, because I seriously freaked out.

Later, when I talked with my friend Eva, I stated that Maiju had seen a completely similar past life to Eva. When I next went to Maiju's energy therapy, she apparently somehow noticed that this had happened and immediately explained that we all have many past lives, some soulmates even have similar ones. I got the feeling that she was explaining too much now, but I ignored it. After that, Maiju didn't talk about any of my past life.

Maiju was also a philanthropist. She collected money for the poor in Egypt and went once a year to deliver the money personally. She always had something "hot" when she returned from her trip.

The people in Maiju's therapies then heard and experienced those fiery events. Maiju said that she lay in the pharaoh's tomb inside the pyramid.
– It's forbidden and dangerous, my friend Eva had told Maiju.
– I know, Maiju had laughed.
– I think it's a violation of the grave peace, I said to Eva. – Can the whole thing even be true, how would tourists get there now, I concluded.
– Yes, Maiju said that someone local had taken her there in such a way that the local guides didn't see, Eva insisted.
  Maiju told me after one of her trips to Egypt that she had been in the desert and charmed a rattlesnake with a local Bedouin.
  Maiju told a great story from the desert at night and how the flames of the campfire rose to a height of meters and the snake also rose. With this ritual, she now had the power of that snake that she used in her energy therapies.
When I was being treated, she explained to me how that huge snake had wrapped itself around her and one end of the therapy table and reached up to the ceiling.
– Great energy, do you feel it, Ella? Maiju asked mesmerized. I felt something strong, but it didn't feel magical, but quite unpleasant.
– Yes, I answered.

Afterwards, I prayed for God's protection for me. I also made the protections taught by Maiju in different colors, because I suspected that Maiju now did not know what she had been dealing with and what could come of it. I couldn't tell Maiju about this because she would surely laugh or consider me a coward.

One time when I was in Maiju's energy healing therapy, Maiju said that my energy field was green, mint green and kerosene green.
– What do they mean? I asked.
– They are the colors of healing, Maiju stated.
– You could heal Ella, she continued.
– Me? I wondered.
– Yes, believe it, Maiju said.
I didn't know how to react, I didn't really like compliments, they always made me feel uncomfortable, but somehow the idea fascinated me.

When I had been Maiju's client for roughly three years, she told me that she was going to organize a course on spiritual matters one more time.
– I am going to share the information that I have received from my own teacher. It is important that this information is shared, but not to just anyone, Maiju said. This would be the last training and she would only take a select few into her group.
– Would you come? Maiju asked me.

I was taken and amazed.
– You have talents Ella, I guess you know that?
– Well, maybe, I answered. My heart was beating
wildly, so I... had I been chosen!!

So Maiju thought of me as a potential healer, and
she certainly got that information from the spirit
world and helpers. I was secretly a little proud.
Now all those supernatural and miraculous events
in my life had an explanation in my mind – I had
talents!

T H R E E

The first training evening was exciting. I had been looking forward to it. I met the five other "chosen ones" and I noticed right away that we all were on the same wavelength.
In addition to me, the other two had quite tough experiences behind them. The other two were gentle women who were interested in the spirit world and the supernatural. We were all Maiju's customers.

I was a little surprised when Maiju started by reading us from her notes. I asked about it, but Maiju was clearly annoyed by my question.
– These notes have been channeled. My teacher Jani has channeled these. Maiju emphasized the word "my".
From the tone of her voice, I concluded that it was not appropriate to ask pointless questions.

First, we studied the Chakra system, its colors, locations and effects. I had never heard of Chakras, and at that time I didn't think to look for any other information about them than what Maiju taught. Chakras had to be learned by heart. Then the protections, which also had to be learned by heart. There were different colors with silver lining and gold edges. I then learned them in the evenings after work.

We learned to hunt for "orbs", i.e. balls of light. They evolved into photographs. They were said to be beings of light in high dimensions. Orbs could appear in the images if the Chakras were open in a certain dimension. Orbs can be angels, unicorns, star helpers, relatives from the spirit world, etc. The feathers found on the road also took on a whole new meaning: They were signs from angels.

We were learning more and more and once I started laughing when the colors of protections were changed once again.

– I'll probably never learn this silver–rimmed pink and then crystal clear, and I won't learn the order either, I once agonized during a course.

– We must protect ourselves better because we are deeper, Maiju instructed.

– You are lights that shine and attract everything, including others in the spirit world, Maiju stated with a staring look in her eyes.

I always noticed whenever I asked something, I annoyed Maiju. She was a teacher who knew her worth and even called us her children and sometimes her sheep. That annoyed me, but I didn't say it out loud.

– How can someone elevate themselves to that position, I thought.

In the next moment, I was already ridding myself of my thoughts. Maybe she was tired, or I disturbed her work.

Once I laughed when Maiju showed us how to move our hands on person lying down and feel the energy.

– Anything can happen here, don't react even if the customer vomits.

– Well, I guess not, I laughed.

I got a look in response that was contemptuous and stinging. Maiju didn't say anything, but I felt bad. I was silent for the rest of the course.

– I have also healed a man in a wheelchair, Maiju said and stood up. – He got up and walked after my energy healing therapy, Maiju declared, and a smug smile spread across her face. We were all silent. I don't know what the others thought, but I had my doubts. However, I decided not to tell others about my doubts. It's not my job to judge.

We had already gathered and healed for each other for a year, studied Chakras, their colors and effects, protections, heard about the underworld, levels of consciousness and much more. Then finally it was time for the time travel course. Maiju always told at the end of the course evening what she would teach us next time. We were all eagerly waiting for the next meeting.

Our families did not understand our studies, so it was best to keep quiet about these things. However, these things spun in our minds more and more.

– We've all been here on earth many times already and now we're going to look at what's hundreds or even thousands of years behind, Maiju began one evening in March.

The purpose was to travel back in time and stop when Maiju said so. She guided our journey with a certain kind of meditation.

I ended up in a dusky hilly dry sandy terrain. I heard moaning and crying from someone. I started walking towards that sound in that desert-like landscape, where I couldn't see well in front of me in the dark. The dry and coarse sand felt still warm underfoot from the hot sun. Everything felt amazingly real, and I felt that space with all my senses. I was clearly somewhere far away, and clearly not in this time. In that twilight I walked behind the hill from which I heard crying and wailing. A strange feeling of sadness came over me and I stayed to watch the situation that was happening very close. I was crouched down and fell to my knees and at the same time started to cry profusely. I saw Jesus on the cross and women weeping at the foot of it. I felt in myself the sorrow of that mother who wept for her son on the cross. Son of God.

– Ella, Ella, come back, Maiju shouted first carefully and then louder.

I found myself sitting in the circle where we always sat in the training.

– Are you okay? Maiju asked and the others looked scared.

– Of course, I said in a daze. Others said that I had fallen from the chair almost to the floor and wailed strangely. I had been in an unnatural position. I didn't really realize the passage of time and I felt like there was no time at all and I was still as if unconscious.

After recovering from this, I told others what I had seen and experienced. Maiju looked at me strangely and there was something in her gaze that I couldn't interpret.

– Well, you can see everything, said Maiju, and I thought I heard contempt in her voice. I didn't understand Maiju's reaction at all, but I didn't stop to think about it.

– What happened here, and can this happen to everyone? – What was this Maiju, explain, explain, the others were amazed and panicked.

– There's nothing to worry about when I'm here,
Maiju said. – But don't try this at home, she
laughed. You travelled to the past.

At some point during those three years, we
practiced having aliens healing of us or through us.
Maiju seemed to like these aliens in particular. She
said she sees these spirits and figures daily and
works with them. Maiju also said that we all have
these aliens in our energy fields.
– They are our helpers or teachers and are always
at our disposal when we want it, Maiju taught.
    After this so-called UFO training, I woke up at
night with a strange feeling in my stomach. I heard
a sound, like an old-fashioned VHS tape being put
into a VCR. The amazing thing was that it also felt
the way it sounded in the stomach. The feeling was
quite strange, I had never experienced anything
like it.
    The next time I went to Maiju for energy healing
therapy, I asked what might have happened or
what this might mean.
– The UFOs have come to take care of you, said
Maiju. – There is no need to be afraid, you only
have one microchip installed.
– What? I snorted a little amused. This annoyed
Maiju.
– You heard right, and be happy, it's not for
everyone, Maiju added.

Maiju also taught us that diamond is an evil stone
and we should try to get rid of all diamonds we
have. She also mentioned that it wouldn't matter if
they were at home or in a safe. Maiju said that the
diamond brings bad luck and death to its wearer,
and if it is somewhere in the house, it must be
disposed of, but not in any way, but in a very
special way.

  Maiju said that she knows how to dispose of
diamonds in a proper way so that the devil can't
get to them anymore. She said if we want to get rid
of our diamonds, we can bring them to her, and
she will bury them in her own backyard. She said
that many of her customers had brought them to
her and she has buried them in a certain place in
her yard with certain ceremonies.

– Thus, they lose their evil power, but they cannot
be dug up, because the evil power returns to them,
Maiju explained seriously.

  Many, she said, had brought her their diamond
rings and other diamond jewelry, and she had done
a great service by burying them. Maiju didn't like
the idea when I asked about burying my own
diamonds in my own yard.

– This is not the same at all, they are still bad, she
said.

I didn't believe this at first and I thought that Maiju
somehow wanted to benefit financially by doing
so. However, I never said this out loud, but later

when we discussed with the other "classmates", we came to the same conclusion.

Maiju was a good storyteller and she made people listen. She always stayed at a distance from us during the training evenings. The distance was both physical and mental. She knew how to create authority and seemed to enjoy the respect it brought.

I have always sensed people's emotional states, also Maiju's and maybe it was a reason she avoided me the most. Later that sensitivity in me got a name. Particularly sensitivity is said to be a characteristic of every Finn. A particularly sensitive person is susceptible to influences, including in my case 100%. I had been like that since early childhood.

Once in Maiju's training the theme was the underworld. I had already canceled that training, but I attended anyway.
– The underworld doesn't sound spiritual at all, how could it possibly be connected to any universal forces and energies. Is it just the opposite? I asked one of my "classmates" on the phone. She had called me about this particular training.

We thought about this together and agreed that this would not belong to the training at all.
– But there is certainly more topics to be discussed as always, Taina said.

So, we decided to participate anyway, we agreed we could leave if we got the feeling that something didn't feel right. Although we both knew that you just can't leave Maiju's training like that. Her very being made us obey.

That evening, Maiju guided us to the underworld. I had no exact idea what the underworld was. Maiju explained that like above, there is also paradise below.
– There are forces in underworld as well as above, this is good for you to remember, Maiju pointed out.

I made a short prayer in my mind before that "journey" because I highly doubted its purpose and as said, I don't think the heaven is under the earth.

Maiju asked us to close our eyes. We had to imagine walking into the forest and finding a hole there. Then we slipped into that hole and travelled to the bottom of the earth. Maiju guided us with her speech on that journey.
I saw a spring and an underground paradise with all its flowers. At the end of the imaginary journey, Maiju said that we can also ask for help from the underworld at any time. It is always available.

– Aren't the folks upstairs enough? I asked. I saw
how Maiju was annoyed by my question.
– Ella! she said fiercely, and that tone of voice
meant stop asking stupid questions.

I got the feeling that she doesn't even know the
answer, and that somehow amused me. In
retrospect, I think she really knew what she was
doing.
   We also learned about retrieving different power
animals from that underworld and different
symbols that we could use to ask for more power
from different spirits.

   We also made a curse cage. Studying that
seemed strange and somehow irrelevant to me, but
I did the work as ordered.

In her free time, Maiju did "cleanings" of homes,
i.e. directed the troublesome spirits into the light.
She also taught that skill to us, her students.
Together we went to different houses to do
cleaning operations.
   In one house, a black, flying and very ugly
"being" met me. It was left spinning on top of us
and when the door was opened it flew out.
– Could it surely come to light now, I thought to
myself. I was also wondering how Maiju was
clearly charmed and laughed in those places. The
rest of us were tense and partly also scared.

Once Maiju asked me to come with her to a house. On the way, I still didn't know what it was about, but when I got there, it became clear.
– What house is this? I asked on the way.
– You'll see, said Maiju.

The house was big and beautiful, but right away in the yard I sensed something unpleasant. The whole yard area was dark, even though there was bright sunshine, and there were hardly any large trees to shade the yard.
When we entered the house, I felt like the interior ceiling was too low. It wasn't really, but I felt that heavy feeling on my shoulders. Inside the house was even darker than outside. That gloom was not caused by the furniture, it was modern and beautiful, as was the rest of the interior. Something in that house made my hair raising.
– This house needs cleaning, Maiju said. – What did you feel Ella?
– Something bad has happened here, I said concerned. I saw corpses in the yard and there was a prisoner in the courtyard building. I told Maiju about what I had "seen" and she nodded.
– Do you see the same? I asked. Maiju was still nodding.
– Then there is a very negative woman who has power. She's bad, really bad, I said.
– Shall we leave here, I asked.

– We can't leave, we have a job to do, Maiju said
demandingly. – We do the Star of David, said
Maiju.
– There are only two of us, I wondered. Maiju had
taught how to make a Star of David, but it required
six people, one for each corner of the triangles.
– It doesn't matter, Maiju said.
I worried in my mind that what is this now, are all
teachings always reversed at some point. We made
that pattern and the associated ceremonies in the
middle of the house.

After that, Maiju wanted to hear more about the
woman I had "seen". We moved to the window
and Maiju asked:
– Do you see that woman now?
– I don't know if I can see, but I feel its closeness,
I said.
– That's right, really close, Maiju said.

I was very intuitive and sensitive with energies. I
also knew how to distinguish between good and
bad. I also often knew what someone was up to.
Now I felt that Maiju called that woman and
pushed it into me. I tried to block that thought in
my mind, Maiju couldn't be that mean. However, I
couldn't get over the feeling and it felt more and
more real.

In my mind, I prayed first to God and then to Jesus. That spirit retreated and Maiju seemed somewhat disappointed.
– Well. Look at the girl, Maiju said.
That convinced me that Maiju had really summoned that spirit and conjured it up on me. What on earth was she up to or was this another test.
I thought about what happened at home and felt anger. I didn't think that was fair or right. At the same time, I thought about how mentioning Jesus in my thoughts made that spirit retreat. This had to be remembered!

Sometimes at the end of training, Maiju invited us to her home for the weekend. We studied nature, trees, their spirits and the different effects of plants.
In the evening, when it was dark, Maiju told us to move on to a slightly more exciting part of our training.
We sat in Maiju's dark living room in the glow of the fireplace, and she asked us to move closer to her.
– I now invite the devil into me, she said pompously.
To me, this didn't seem good thing at all, and many participants thought the same at the time, when we discussed the matter later.

We were all speechless, stunned and amazed at the same time. But as said, we had already noticed by now that it was not possible or worthwhile to oppose Maiju.

We were all too kind in some way and believed in her and that she wants the best for us. I prayed to Jesus Christ in my mind when Maiju started to change.

Maiju's face distorted, and her eyes turned red. They shined in that twilight, and she resembled a monster. I couldn't believe my eyes. Maiju looked creepy and scary, and it was hard for me to believe what I was seeing, but I had to because I saw it with my own eyes and those others saw the same.

In the middle of us sat someone who resembled a monster from a horror movie. Was this our great spiritual teacher, I thought. There was something totally evil there.

Gradually, Maiju returned to normal and looked at us in wonder. She pretended she didn't know what happened. I didn't believe her words at all.

Maiju later explained that this was important for our development. In her opinion, it was good for us to face evil as well, so that we are not surprised if it ever comes and that we recognize it. She grinned when she saw our scared and horrified expressions. I got the feeling she was enjoying the situation.

– Do you still dare to sleep? she smiled.

I didn't want to spend the night under the same roof with that "creature".

That was the end of Maiju's training, but I continued to attend her energy healing therapies.

FOUR

The death of my brother Tapani touched me deeply. He was seriously ill for a long time but persevered for many years. When he was transferred to hospice care, I visited him several times, even though he lived far north in another town.

One evening in November, I felt like I had to go to him first thing in the morning. I sent a message to my supervisor that I had to go and that I would be taking an unpaid day off. I left on the first train.

Tapani was in the hospital for a pain pump replacement, and I noticed right away that his condition had worsened since last time. I fed him and talked, raised the pillow and tried to make him feel better.

Then when it came time for him to take the ambulance back to the terminal care, he said he couldn't make it. I went near him and hugged him. He said in a weak voice that he wanted to listen to music.

I put the small radio inside the pillow near him. Then I prayed in my mind:
– If God exists, make this dear person feel better. Only a moment passed and then my brother went to his heavenly home.

When I went to Maiju's therapy full of sadness and told what had happened, Maiju asked:
– When exactly did your brother go on a journey to heaven? I told Maiju the day and time.
– He came to greet me right after that, Maiju said.

I felt that my brother had no reason to visit Maiju and the whole idea annoyed me. Did Maiju want to score points for someone's death.
– Your abilities will deepen, Maiju said.
That didn't comfort me, but made me feel guilty, because in Maiju's opinion, the death of a loved one always opens new doors to deeper spirituality and understanding.

Later, when my mother fell ill and her condition worsened, Maiju said something unimaginably cruel. – You have the opportunity to develop again.

– What?? I asked, dismayed. – Do you mean that I
will develop more when my mother sleeps away? I
continued ironically. I was filled with holy anger.
How could someone talk like that!
Maiju didn't seem to understand the irony and
contempt that I also showed. She just answered
convincingly and slowly – Yes.
– Oh, that death is a commodity, right? I couldn't
control myself anymore.
Maiju seemed to be grinning and that made me
boil inside even more. – If that's what you want to
say, she said, still with a grin on her face.

   Even after that I went back to her. If only the
spirit world had a special mission for me, and
Maiju seemed to know something more about it
than I did.

Maiju offered me her own therapy room for a
reasonable fee so that I could practice my skills.
She herself was away for a long time at the time
and promised to recommend me to her own clients.

My first energy therapy client was coming for
energy healing therapy, and I had already been
excited about it throughout my working day. I got
home from work at four and took a quick shower
and changed clothes. I didn't want to carry any
"rush energy" with me in my clothes. Maiju had
taught this too.

I opened the trunk of my car and put my bag, blanket, and pillow in there. At the same time, the trunk lid came loose from its springs and fell directly on top of my head. Blood poured down my face and I felt dizzy. My first thought was that someone or something is trying to stop me from leaving, but I pushed the thought aside because it was already a rush.

After a while I regained my balance, ran back home, wet the towel with cold water and pressed it against my head. There was no time for this now. I had to go because my first client was coming.

I stopped the blood supply and set off.
At Maiju's therapy room, I cleaned up more and prepared everything for the energy healing therapy. I made the protections according to Maiju's instructions and asked the universe for help so that I wouldn't bleed, and everything would go well.

The customer was really demanding, and she talked all the time. I felt like I couldn't concentrate at all. The customer asked all the time what I saw or felt. I told her that I act differently than Maiju and that we will talk when the energy therapy is over. The client was not satisfied with my method and started comparing it to Maiju's therapy.
– She promised that this will follow the same formula, the customer complained to me. – Maiju promised me, she continued. – This is not at all what I am used to, she continued. – Couldn't you do like Maiju, she asked.

– I have my own way of doing things, but it's not necessarily worse, just different, I tried to explain and felt myself sweating.

I was panicking and annoyed at the same time. Maiju could have told me how to deal with this client.

I had specifically asked if there was anything I should know so that I could serve her as well as possible.

– No way, Maiju had laughed.

I was angry with Maiju, and I felt that she wanted me to fail. That client never came to me again. This was also the beginning of this career, but I didn't get discouraged.

I started doing energy healing therapies at my home and Maiju was clearly upset about it. She often said that since I was her student and learned from her, I could rent her premises. I still went to her energy healing therapy, and she talked to me about it several times. However, I wanted to decide my own affairs.

I felt the urge to try something completely different from time to time, and I started meeting different kinds of spiritual people. They had been to India and talked about a Centre there where you can get enlightened.

That enlightenment would take a month and a man from this group had been there. When you come home, you should stay completely alone and preferably in the dark for three days and only then meet other people and go out.
– It sounds unbelievable, I wouldn't believe it if I didn't know that man, who was highly educated and quite intelligent, I thought.

Deeksha method was also taught at that Centre, and Finns had been taught there.

Deeksha was said to have healing energy. (Much later I heard that getting it would bring about a rise in spiritual level, a rise in social and religious status so much that even the richest person would bow down to you).

Those who visited those centers in India had seen white spirits hovering around them in that area of the Centre when they were awake, and it was said to be completely normal there. This really piqued my interest.

I started dreaming about a trip to India and to that Centre. I just didn't have the money for it, the trip would take a month and cost three thousand euros.

When Deeksha's method course next arrived in my own town, I found myself there. I didn't know what wonderful force was taking me all the time towards something new. At that time, I still didn't know what could be behind all of this.

The couple who taught that Deeksha method was like a newly-in-love couple on a honeymoon. They were in their fifties and all smiles in their white robes. They both used the Hindi name they got in India, but to me they were Minna and Mauri. The couple told our group their own stories of their enlightenment in India.

We did many breathing exercises during the weekend, which were extremely difficult to do. For almost ten minutes we had to hoke the sentence that read in Hindi on the blackboard. No breaks were allowed.

The second exercise was a hard inhale and a hard exhale. Then we rolled around on the floor and went to a pre-selected childhood trauma or difficult situation. We were asked to shout that feeling out.

Many cried inconsolably, and so did I. Then we got to rest for half an hour. We course members were asked not to meet anyone that day when we left the course.

I drove several ten kilometers from that course by car to return home the next day, and I was lucky on the way, because I don't remember anything about the whole trip.
I was in a confused state and eventually wondered what I was doing in the backyard.

In retrospect, I have thought that I was truly blessed on the trip. After I got home, I was as if in a dream all evening and went to bed early.

The next morning, I drove back and then we were initiated as Deeksha's mediators. Once or twice, I was conveying Deeksha to a spiritual group. We placed our hands on the head or shoulders of these people and the Deeksha flowed.

The passion of traveling to India dissipated when that man I knew had been to that Centre for the second time.
– Aren't you enlightened? I asked a little sarcastically. He didn't like my question. He said

that the Centre in question also organizes rapid lighting courses. It would only take 6 days but cost a few thousand more than a month's course.

After that, my interest in that Centre stopped completely. – Why is there always money somehow involved in all these spiritual things, I wondered in my thoughts.
– What Jesus did was always free. Isn't that true spirituality, I wonder.

Maiju was also of the opinion that India should be forgotten.

After that, though, I went to hug Mother Amma, or actually Mother Amma hugs first. I waited for that hug for several hours and finally on my knees for the last 15 minutes. Amma whispered something in my ear, and it was then interpreted elsewhere. It didn't bother me that Mother Amma was of a different religion than me.

New Age includes the fact that there can be several gods, anything goes. At the time, I myself was of the opinion that there is only one God, but different people name God in different ways. Well, for example, there are millions of Hindu gods, but I didn't think about that at the time.

S I X

A few years passed and I had earned a name as an energy healer. People came to me with problems, and I wanted to help everyone from the bottom of my heart. People had problems everywhere and for those who had a lot of pain in their past, I felt quite helpless. They said they would get help, but the feeling of inadequacy and sadness overwhelmed me, e.g. when dealing with customers who have experienced incest, violence and abuse. I always asked them to contact professionals. I started praying at night for those clients, it felt right, but I decided to keep it to myself.

Maiju advised me not to think too much, they are just customers. In Maiju's opinion, those things should be forgotten when closing the door to the therapy room. I didn't think it could go that way and decided to ignore Maiju's advice. Maiju herself addressed her customers as her loved ones, and hugged them as they left, but something in her sent chills down my skin.

I once found to my amazement that I was able to connect with other people's spirit guides easily. I had read a lot of literature about them and looked up information on the Internet, but I didn't think I would be able to get in touch with them.
I sat down and put my hands in my lap. As with almost any New Age ceremony or contact, I opened my palm up. Then the energy would flow correctly. I closed my eyes, concentrated, asked the highest power and the universe for help, and called the spirit guides present to me. I felt someone's presence and asked if she was my friend Sari's spirit guide. I got an affirmative answer. I asked Sari for a symbol and a message. I saw the symbol clearly before my closed eyes and a message to Sari was brought to my consciousness. It was just one word. I had agreed with Sari about it, and she was very happy when she heard about this.

I started paint the symbols on the stones I collected and gave them to my friends as talismans. I also sold a few when word got around.
   All kinds of symbols flashed in my eyes and messages came at a furious pace.

Then I thought I'd also ask for a sign for myself. I concentrated and a strange feeling came over me. I got a symbol with some sort of letter Y that resembled the letter J. I didn't get the message, but I got a name for the symbol: Yeshua. I thought that name was beautiful and special. I didn't think about the origin of the name anymore and the Bible was quite unknown to me at the time.

However, one day I started googling that name and was very surprised. The name meant the Hebrew name of Jesus. At that time, I thought that the spirit world was playing with me, because I can't have Jesus as a spirit guide, no one can. I thought you were blasphemy, because Jesus was never one of the risen masters to me, but much more. I didn't know how to place Jesus in the frame of New Age, even though I believed God was working there.

The triune concept of God, which I had heard about, was foreign to me. I had certainly heard about God, the son of God and the Holy Spirit, but I did not understand or care about their connection. They were all true to me, but fifteen years of immersion in New Age had clouded the perception badly.

Now I know that that was already a sign of Jesus at that time. A sign of how He was ready to offer me salvation, but I did not understand it. Someone else might say it was an attempt by the spirit

powers to fool me, but I think it was something else.
That name caused a deep longing in me, an indescribable longing that brought tears to my eyes.

S E V E N

Then my dear mother passed away.

I had helped many when facing death and told how death is not the end.
Now my life seemed to end with my mother's death. A great sadness came over me.

I had asked in prayer that I would be by my mother's side when she left for her last journey, and my request came true. I managed to hold her hand for an hour before she left.

Nothing I learned comforted me now and my expectations were high when I went to Maiju again for energy therapy.

– Oh, my sheep, Maiju said when she saw me and spread her arms for a hug. I hugged her and cried, but I also bit my teeth thinking that what a sheep I am to you. Maiju told the same story again as when my brother died.

– Your mother visited here before she left for heaven. She is now in a state where she goes through her life as if watching a movie, Maiju continued.

Maiju had taught us that after death we go to that state where we look back at our lives like in a movie theater. Then we would be able to learn and come back, because a person must learn a lot and come back many times before being enlightened and entering the eternal light.

Shortly after that, Maiju's good friend and spiritual guru, who used Tarot cards in his sessions, came to visit Maiju's therapy room. I made an appointment with him, and he told me with his cards that I have experienced sadness, I am training, and the future will bring change.

That session would subconsciously guide my life choices because I believed in what the guru said. Guru had known about my grief and that was a clear sign that what he said was worth trusting.

I had met Marika at Maiju's course, who sent me a message shortly after my mother's death. Marika had heard about my mother's passing and decided to contact me. In the message, she said that she knew the famous psychic medium Leila, who was coming to our city. There would be a limited number of sessions and she had thought I might want an appointment.

– Yes, make an appointment for me, I answered immediately. I missed her very much and wanted to connect with my mother.

When the day finally came when Leila, that famous psychic medium, arrived in my hometown, I was stiff with excitement. I wrote some questions on paper so I wouldn't forget anything. I had been instructed not to record anything.

Leila was a small elderly woman with dark eyes and a peculiar voice. I waited my turn on a chair placed in the hotel corridor, and my legs didn't want to stay still. Finally, the door opened ajar. No one came to ask me in, so I cautiously peeked through the door.

– Just come, the medium said in her rough voice and motioned for me to sit down. She looked me over, tilted her head and smiled.

– There is a young thin man sitting next to you, he comes really close, so he is close to you. Do you know him? Leila asked.

– Um, is he dead, I asked in my confusion. I had never been to a medium session before.

– Yes, he has moved to the spirit world at a young age, Leila continued.

– He is my brother, I said confused.

– Your brother is pleased that you are here, the medium said.

Then it was mom's turn. Leila couldn't get in touch with her properly, but said she saw her. Leila said that my mother is still in the state we are in immediately after death.

– What's the condition, is she all right? I was in a hurry. – Yes, she is all right, Leila said and smiled.

I cried and tried my best to swallow so I wouldn't cry out loud.

When the session was over, Leila said that she would organize a self-knowledge course in a nearby town, which would discuss e.g., negative thought patterns and beliefs. Some people would be included, and the course would not be open to everyone.

– You would fit in well, Leila said and continued:
– You should act quickly, because these courses are in demand.

I felt like I was lost with myself especially right now. I somehow mourned a lot. It would be good for me to learn more about myself. – Do I even know myself well enough, I thought.
– I could go along.
– Then inform to Marika right away, Leila said.

I did the work as told and was excited about the new course and developing myself. If only I could learn something new about myself.

The self-knowledge course began, and Leila told everyone something very personal for everyone to hear, something that no one could know. She didn't reveal everything, but just enough to surprise us all.

She had a hold of us. I got the feeling that she knew what we would need. Several of us opened about our own problems and weaknesses, but for some it was insurmountable.

During that six-month course, we all got to know each other and shared painful life experiences.

Leila often hid the answer to her questions and made us admit things we wanted to hide.

In a way, Leila was also distant, scary and she had authority over us. Somehow afterwards I felt that she broke our shell. For some it was too much, and they were about to drop out of the course. Marika was able to talk a few back.

In retrospect, I have stated to myself that all of us course participants had a lot in common; we all had some inner wound – the wound of being rejected, which manifested itself in many ways.

When Maiju heard that I had attended Leila's course, she was completely shocked. She looked dismayed but said nothing. I felt that she could not bear the thought of me and her other students seeking education elsewhere. I knew that Maiju would still tease me about that.

The self-knowledge course was coming to an end and Marika came to me one day and said that Leila had told her that I had skills to become a psychic medium. The course would soon start in another town. Marika knew that I didn't want to drive long distances, so she promised in the same breath that I would get her ride when I came.

Marika had trained as a psychic medium herself and I had been interested and asked her about the subject. However, I was surprised by the fact that

you could train for it. I had thought it was a gift
from birth.

However, I hesitated to go down that path
myself, there was something fascinating about it
on the one hand, and something scary on the other.
I mentioned it to Marika, and she was amused:
– We are helpers, there is nothing scary about it.
Marika asked me to get back to it as soon as
possible, because the training would start soon.

After thinking about it for a few days, I sent
Marika a message: – Okay, I'm in. What next?
Marika answered quickly. She would give me
private instruction as I would have to take a basic
course in spiritual awareness. The education given
by Maiju did not meet the criteria of the spiritualist
society, so it had to be completed before the basic
medial course.

That course included the Chakra system and
many things that I already knew, so it was mostly
rushed through and passed. I personally didn't like
that kind of thoroughness, but now was busy.

In the basic mediumship course, there were about ten of us at the beginning.

As a teacher, I think Leila was old-school strict and, in this training, we got a "cold shower" every time. Leila got angry if someone didn't listen and seemed to be more in a bad mood than even moderately good. I felt like she downright despised us from time to time.

Most of the time it felt like we were being "checked out" and had earned the teacher's indignation and unkindness. It bothered me immensely. How can a great spiritual teacher be mean-spirited. I asked Marika about it one time when we were driving home.

– That's just Leila's style, you shouldn't be offended by it. Besides, working with the spirit world can sometimes be difficult, Marika said.

– It's probably so, I answered, although I didn't think that was a sufficient explanation. Marika herself was always calm, even though Leila scolded her with harsh words.

Well, I couldn't know about Leila's reasons, so I tried to forget about it. On the one hand, I respected her and wished her well, but she was not very receptive.

In the mediumship training, we did not only message delivery but also clairvoyance exercises. We read things about water, fabrics, plants and just about anything.

Once, at the beginning of the training, we did an exercise where you had to read something about the life of the person sitting across from you. At that time, we didn't know each other yet, so the exercise was a challenge. However, I felt that it was easy for me. I told Maija, who was sitting in front of me, that she worked in a big white house with many floors and many windows and that she took care of children. I also told that her late father was Veikko, and he wore certain kind of clothes.

Maija said that she worked in the hospital's children's ward and her father Veikko had died, but at the time he liked to dress exactly as I had described.

Later, I had a lot of successes and sensed a lot of things. I gradually became convinced that my connection to the spirit world was working.

Every time I came home from those training days, my family said I was weird. I was irritable and on my own. On the one hand, my conscience was knocking, because I had just been away and my family would have missed me, and on the other hand, I thought that when I develop more, I can give my family more as well.

When I told Maiju that I'm in psychic medium training, she was blown away. Her disappointment was visible from afar.

– I would never train as a psychic medium, she said contemptuously. Maiju never seemed to be happy for me, it made me sad.

My medium training was about halfway through, when Maiju decided to keep charity event in her therapy room.

– You can also participate, Maiju said.

I hadn't promised anything, but I didn't dare refuse either. She had already prepared an ad and told her clients that a psychic medium would be there. I got angry because I wasn't a medium yet, and I wasn't ready by any means. However, I knew that this was now Maiju's revenge. She wanted me to fail.

Maiju had reserved seven clients for me, and the money would go to charity. I was terrified; how could I do it.

– I'm not ready, and I shouldn't appear as a medium yet, I said. Maiju grinned at my fear.

– Yes, you can, you are trained.

I was nervous when the first customer arrived.

I contacted the spirit world as I had been taught.
I got in touch with the client's deceased relative,
who I then described to the client. The customer
recognized that relative and it was time to receive
a message from the newcomer. The message was
clear.

The next one went perfectly, but I felt a little
strange.
– Oh no, five more, I thought. I asked the spirit
world for help so that I could cope. I was able to
forward the messages to everyone and the
customers were satisfied.

After that I slept all weekend. I was totally
exhausted. Maiju didn't comment on the matter
when I told her how exhausted I was after the
sessions. I knew myself that I had crossed my
limit, and I was by no means ready.

However, I was surprised by how the Messaging
really taxed my strength.

Then came the evening in the mediumship studies,
when there were general rehearsals for the medium
event and there were members of the club in the
audience.

Leila had taught that at the beginning of the
event, the opener reads the Our Father prayer. It
was not heard now, nor in previous training
sessions. I asked Marika about this too, when I
didn't dare to ask Leila, like neither did the others.
– He will probably read it herself, Marika assured.
But I was not convinced.

Leila instructed that we should trust the spirit that comes and listen to it. Not making up our own. She got extremely angry if she caught someone doing that.
– You seem to forget that I can see if you lie, Leila shouted.

Then finally it was the turn of the actual medium event open to the public and we got into a real situation.
  I felt sorry for one Hanna, who started talking about the boat, the reeds and the lake.
– What the hell are you talking about, Leila snarled and stormed onto the stage. – Now get down to business, she continued to set things up.
– When people don't understand, they didn't come here to listen to fairy tales, she snapped in front of everyone, rolling her eyes and smiling confidently at the audience.
  I felt so bad for the embarrassed Hanna that my anger started to rise. Hanna was unable to continue, and Leila rushed back to the stage.
– Well, don't you see that event or who it concerns, she snapped.
– A person has drowned here, Leila "saved" the situation and Hanna was able to understand the message brought by the spirit.
  When that medium event was over, Leila angrily shouted at all of us. My anger took over. She had no right to set us up like that!

We all left the event with regret, and at the same time I decided that I am not going to participate in the further course.

Mediumship activities include organizing a "spiritual circle" and working in it regularly.
 I participated in circles organized by others for half a year and one time, when we were practicing contacting the dead, something strange happened. It was about going into a trance, that is, you had to let the spirit take over you, and move aside. The idea seemed unpleasant to me, but I did the exercise according to the instructions.
– Ella, Ella, someone shouted.
– Come back, come back now, someone still shouted demandingly. I was still sitting in my chair and the others were staring amazed.
– Is everything okay, the circle leader asked.
– Well, yes, I answered. – What happened? I asked. I had a vague recollection of someone speaking, but I couldn't understand the language.
– You spoke some strange language, the circle leader said.
– You went into a trance before I even noticed and it was hard for you to come back, she continued.
 The others who participated in that circle did not want to practice trance after that. I freaked out too. I didn't like the idea of something taking over me and talking through my mouth, and I couldn't do anything.

I then became the convener and leader of the spiritual circle in my area. I organized a spiritual circle for a couple of years until I felt it was time to leave it.

I didn't like the feeling of leading others, and yet others expected it. In addition, that took up my short free time anyway, which was all away from my family.

I also participated in a few self-knowledge courses organized by Leila. I don't think I was with myself yet, and when Leila called, I felt like she knew that I needed a course. After all, she is a clairvoyant and a psychic medium!

In those courses, most of the day was spent sitting, listening and answering. Leila read the texts she channeled and the doctrines she prepared for us. We also did different exercises.

At times we were like in a torture chamber when Leila kept things from us that we would not have wanted to open about.

I had enough of those courses as well, when Leila got angry and was yelling there as well. It was unreasonable to me. Some continued even after that.

When people heard that I had been in psychic medium training, they wanted to make appointment to my seatings and therapies.

I did energy healing therapy and made some spiritual messaging also if the client so desired. Customers also always wanted to know things about the future. I often saw things that happened to them symbolically.

An unknown woman came to me for energy healing therapy, and I saw the drawings of the building in glowing red. When I mentioned that, she was surprised to say that the drawings of the new home had been made for them that very day, but the old home was still unsold, and it caused them a lot of trouble.

A couple I've known for a long time came to talk to me because their house was haunted. That couple had long been interested in New Age and everything related to it. The ghosts themselves didn't bother them, but they couldn't invite guests, not to mention night guests. They said that the ghosts made a noise that made the guests wonder.

I promised to do two distance cleanings for their home, and they said afterwards that the ghosts disappeared.

A client came in for energy healing therapy and when I grabbed his hand, I felt a really heavy sensation. I felt as if the ceiling was weighing on my shoulders and a name came to mind: Minna. I told the client about this, and he sat up and told me that his aunt Minna is an extremely heavy and dark person who tried to impose on him in every way.

I started to see people's energies right from the people walking on the street and I also distinguished those who had some heavy sadness with them.

I also singled out those who had strayed to the "wrong side," as they were called.

However, not all new agers believed there could be spiritual people who are "in the grip of evil". It was clear to me, because I felt, saw and even heard the existence of that evil from some persons. Such a person under the influence of evil appeared to me inside a gray veil. Even if that person was a few meters away from me, I couldn't make out his face behind that dark curtain. Some looked and felt completely black.

Once I was driving a car and I felt "evil" in my neck. It felt disgusting and smelled evil, I knew it was black energy. I wondered where it came from until I looked in the transom. A gang member dressed in black was hanging out on my bumper with a thick-wheeled motorcycle. I could feel that person's anger. And I knew that my driving according to the speed limit had annoyed him heavily. Then he started to pass quickly on a narrow road.

I once jogged in pitch darkness with only a headlamp as my light. It was an October evening, and my jogging path was in the countryside, and there were no streetlights anywhere near. While jogging there, I felt something "bad" far away from me. I continued my journey on foot. Suddenly that "evil" was right next to me. It came in seconds behind my back. The feeling was unpleasant. I remembered Maiju's advice that I shouldn't feel fear. I wasn't very brave, but I decided not to be afraid. It didn't take long before that "evil" nearby left.

Later, when I told Maiju about what happened, she said that we course members are being tested.

I once unknowingly annoyed a self-respecting woman when I refused to teach her distance healing. She was not used to objections, and I got to know her anger afterwards. She had told me earlier about an acquaintance of her who controlled the energies of electronic devices. I knew she had put a curse on me because my TV would turn off and on by itself and my brand new and expensive speakers would turn up the volume without adjusting. The service did not find anything wrong with the equipment.

A man who taught Reiki slept in a coffin. It was said that he had turned to evil. Evil was said to attract and flatter, praise and praise, and therefore it was easy to fall into its trap. Fortunately, I recognized these evil-worshipping parties and tried to stay away from them.

T E N

It was 2017 and my childhood friend Sari had heard about a healer who had healed some of her acquaintances. Her mother's knee and her aunt's shoulder.

– Shall we go there? Sari asked excitedly. She wanted to get help for her stomach problems.

– They say it's a sectarian, but I guess that doesn't matter, Sari continued.

– Oh no, a believer? I asked a little hesitantly.

– Yes, Sari said.

– Well, is he trying to convert at the same time and is he a Jehovah's Witness? I asked.

– Well, I don't think so, mother and aunt would have talked about it, Sari explained.

I was afraid of being bullied more than anything, and I had an experience from childhood of people belonging to a certain sect, who came to our house after my father died and cried for my mother. Mom was crying inconsolably, and I was scared. I hated those people then.

This healer mentioned by Sari had facilities in another town and I had to wait a long time for his therapy.

We were able to book consecutive appointments from him for the same day a month later.

Sari and I drove to the therapy together, a little nervous. I was the first to be treated.

This man was about 70 years old and had a big dog in his therapy room. I scared the dog at first, but the man said it was nice. There was also a large TV in the room, the loudness of which bothered me a bit.

I was dressed to long-sleeved underwear, as the healer had instructed on the phone. I went to lie down on the therapy table, and he asked about my ailments.
I told him about my early onset menopause, and it made him mumble.

– Does it hurt? the healer asked and pressed a point on the inside of the foot.

– Not exactly, I answered. I was treated from the back and different parts of the body.

– How did you become a healer? dare I ask. The man said that he had been to the service of the local Pentecostal church and that an evangelist had given him the gift of a healer through prophecy. I didn't fully understand what he meant, but I remember thinking at the time that it was a gift from God. I then reacted happily:

– I am also an energy healer.

– It's from the devil! the man roared in response.

That answer pissed me off immensely and I shouted in my mind: – IT'S NOT!!

And at the same time there was a loud crash, the television went off, all the lights went dark, and the electricity went out.

– That's what you got, I thought.

– Now what is this, the healer wondered.

After a while, the lights came back on, and the power came back on.

I was quite sure that my helpers in the spirit world came to show that man that he was wrong. (Later I thought about it differently).

The situation was a little uncomfortable, so I decided it was best to change the subject. I talked about other things, and we were on "neutral ground" again.

Then I asked the man if I could tell him about a dream that stuck in my mind.

– Go ahead, the man said.

I told about a dream I had seen some months before. In that dream, yellow men dressed in tin armor were marching in hundreds of thousands across the entire world map.

– They are Chinese, the healer said. – But they won't come yet, but in a few years. That's where it comes from, he continued thoughtfully.

When Corona started spreading from China in 2020, I vividly remembered that dream and the healer's words. Had I seen a premonition…

My friend Sari wanted to go to that healer again and she did, but I refused.

I didn't get help for my ailments; they would have required more visits. And I felt that I wasn't welcome anymore, and I didn't want to see him anymore.

ELEVEN

New Age people were shocked in 2017 when the New Age guru Doreen Virtue converted to Christianity. Every energy healer I know had access to some of Doreen's material, either angel cards or literature.

There was a lot of buzz about it, many people got rid of all the cards and books she had published. For me, that was a turning point: If Doreen Virtue, a great influencer and creator of the angel therapy system, did something like that, there had to be something right about it.

Doreen Virtue made angel therapy a big business over the course of 10 years, and now she has started to speak out against all of it.

I tried to start a discussion on the subject among my spiritual friends, but no one wanted to talk about it more deeply. Many had an opinion that Doreen was completely delusional and did not know what she was doing.

However, she ruined her own business.

– There had to be some bigger truth behind that
courage, I concluded.

Once, while doing an energy therapy, I was sure I
was going to pass out. My legs were weak, and I
could barely stand. My client at the time was a
really sick old lady and her legs were so bad she
could barely walk.
   When I asked Maiju about it, she said that I get
tired because I give my own energy.
   I often felt the pains and ailments of the people I
treated in my body, but I thought there was more
to the matter. I felt like I wasn't listening to my
inner self, but the feeling got buried in everything I
was doing. I was pushing forward like a steam
locomotive.
   That same old woman also asked me for distance
energy therapy, and I promised to send it to her in
the evenings.
   Soon I had a lot of names to whom I transmitted
distance energy for free in the evenings and the
recipients were satisfied.
   However, that debilitating feeling continued, and
I went to measure my blood levels. Everything was
fine except for the kidney value. I couldn't
understand what has caused this suddenly. The
doctor couldn't find an explanation either, just
stated that the situation is being monitored.

I discussed the matter once with a woman who had
a long experience with New Age. I told her about

my kidney values. She asked me if I knew that mediumship, and these spiritual abilities related to New Age, affect the endocrine system and especially the kidneys and thyroid gland. I really didn't know. But I knew that at least five psychic mediums and a few clairvoyants I knew had hypothyroidism.

That information scared me, but I thought that I was still in God's work and protection.
From time to time the thought came to my mind and I decided to visit the laboratory every year to measure my values.

TWELVE

There are several psychic schools in Great Britain where you can study mediumship or otherwise develop your spiritual skills.

Spiritualism is said to be the eighth largest religion in UK, they have their own churches and congregations widely across United Kingdom.
  These schools run by spiritualists attract people from all over the world, and even from Finland many people interested in spiritual things go to these training centers for courses and seminar weeks.

  Mediums who have graduated from these training centers or who teach in them often visit all over Europe and in Finland too.

I was asked to join such a 10-day intensive course in UK and I decided to go. I was excited once again and set off with a few of my other New Age friends.

I was very surprised at the airport, because I noticed that there were a lot of like-minded people leaving Finland. Suddenly there were more than 50 of us going to UK to learn and develop our intellectual and medial abilities.

In the toilet queue of the plane, I came to chat with a middle-aged woman. I asked her where she was going.
– Well, I don't really know. I don't remember the name of that place, she answered thoughtfully.
– Was it like this and I mentioned the name of the course place where I was on my way.
– Yes, I guess it was, she nodded.
– Do you know what is being done there? I asked the woman.
– Not really, my friend told me that it's worth going there now. She told me that great things are happening there, the woman answered.

I was totally confused and asked her if she really doesn't know where she is going and what she is participating in.
– I don't know, answered the woman.
That thing bothered me a lot. There was a large group of us going to UK for spiritualistic courses, and there were certainly many who had no idea where they were going.

When we then arrived at that wonderful old manor-like building, we all admired everything we saw almost in unison. The beautifully worn building was like something out of a movie with its charming gardens and large rooms.

Cows roamed the adjacent meadow and behind it a river flowed quietly.

Inside the building, it felt as if we had travelled back in time a couple of hundred years. Large plush carpets covered the dark lacquered floors, and on the high walls hung large gilt wide-edged paintings depicting dignitaries and beautiful landscapes.

The building had belonged to a rich family and was now under the control of a spiritualist society. After checking in, we were given our room, which was at the top of many creaking stairs, around several corners.

The staff and translators were extremely friendly and it made me feel at home.

Translators were needed, because we were from many countries and not everyone understood English.

At the same time, there was something about the place that was both appealing and mysteriously

mystical, and genuine and original. I was excited
and at the same time very nervous.

The school curriculum was quite strict; it started
at nine in the morning and ended at nine in the
evening. In between we ate well, and the teachers
said that we should eat well to ground ourselves,
because we are dealing with very high-flying
things.

We were divided into groups based on what we
are interested in. Not everyone got into the group
they were interested in, but the teachers chose their
own students according to their own intuition.
I was selected as Paul's student.

Paul was a very successful business owner who
had experienced a spiritual awakening
coincidentally with his leg pain. He had been
seeing a spiritualist healer who had said Paul had a
bigger mission in life than his successful business.
Paul was a good-natured man, easy-going and
calm – a completely different kind of teacher than
what I was used to in Finland. Paul spoke calmly
and didn't have any notes.

We spent hours in his training, and he always
spoke without any papers, books or notes. He
seemed to be speaking under the guidance of
something.

Not everyone in our group understood English, so we also had an interpreter there.

I was in a group that practiced healing. I had a strange feeling from the beginning of the course, which got stronger all the time. That something seemed to take me somewhere at high speed.
This spiritual healing course seemed absolutely fascinating to me, but still something about it raised doubts. I wondered to myself if this is all about God as they say.

We had received the program of the course. Each day had its own program, and I noticed a Divine Service marked for each evening.

– Well, we are definitely on the right track here, I thought when I saw that.

On the evening of the first day, when that service came, all of us, nearly 70 people, gathered in the sanctuary, which was on the ground floor of that wonderful old building.
The sanctuary had many chairs and a performance stage in front and a speaker's booth. When we arrived at that shrine, all the teachers, or psychic mediums, were there and they were sitting next to each other on the stage in front.

I had expected a traditional service, but the truth dawned on me very soon.

One of the mediums stood up and selected music to play in the background. The music track was a beautiful song by a famous English pop musician and was followed by other similar tracks. We didn't pray, sing hymns or anything else that belongs to a traditional service, instead the whole service was a psychic medium event.

Mediums took turns receiving messages from the spirit world and the recipient was always found. I also received a very specific message from my mother. The psychic medium who delivered that message described things that only I knew about my mother. I was dumbfounded.

I'm also a bit confused by this strange service, which to me was a mockery of God. I then thought that this is how it goes with them.

One thought stuck in my mind: was this about God? God was mentioned many times, and it was also written in the seven principles of spiritualists that were on the wall boards.

Those principles mentioned e.g. that: God is our Father and there are no other fathers. And that God is light, power and love.

Other principles were everyone is our sister and brother, the soul continues to live after the death of the physical body, connection with the spirit world is possible, everyone is personally responsible for their actions, what we sow in this world, we will reap in the future, and the path of each soul's development is eternal.

Jesus was not mentioned anywhere, because spiritualists do not believe in a resurrected Jesus.

Spiritualists consider contact with the spirit world and communication with them as their main principle.

Paul taught us to "travel" through meditation to the spirit world and encounter the light. With the help of that meditation, we learn to let go of our thoughts and let go of everything. We experienced and saw that light and Paul guided us. He said that light is God. Those exercises felt powerful. I try to do everything exactly as Paul taught.

– Ella why are you resisting? Paul wondered.
– You resist all the time. We have a great spirit in this group; absolutely brilliant spirit, everyone accepts it, but you resist.
– Why? Spirit wants you to join Ella, you have talents, you have talents, whatever Ella! I could see you here teaching again. They want you in, why are you resisting? Are you afraid?
– No, I answered. – Or I don't know.

I was also a little ashamed, because I felt like a traitor to the group. Something in me resisted, and at the time I didn't know what it was. Something didn't seem right. We did the same exercise several times a day and it started to feel better. That light I encountered was so bright it had to be from God. I began to be convinced of that.

That light was like a great shining angel leading to a greater light.
I finally got into that meditation; wonderful energy flooded everywhere, it enveloped. Time lost its meaning, presence was here, now.

– Is the enlightenment like this? I thought.

Then Paul said we could try a little trance. It wasn't part of this course, but he wanted to give us a small taste of what it could be, because next year there would also be a course on trance. We might have a chance to participate if we were interested.

Paul guided us all into a state where we went into a trance, or some of us did, some of us didn't.
By state here I mean the state of mind or mental state that the trance medium falls into when doing a trance. The trance medium hands over his body to the use of the spirit and withdraws himself to the side.
I experienced falling into a trance very strongly and suddenly an insanely strong pain cut through my chest. I thought I was going to die. I gasped and was scared. I have never experienced such intense pain as what was cutting through my chest.

I tried to say something, but I couldn't, I was still
panting and hoping that someone would notice
what was happening to me. But no one seemed to
notice anything, and no wonder, because
everyone's eyes were closed.

After that trance exercise was over, we had to go
eat. I did not recover from that condition; I was
very slow, and my speech was slow, I was in a
completely different world, and everything felt
unreal. At the same time, I was scared that I would
go back to my old self, and sad that I had given
away control.
After a few hours I was back to normal. Later I ask
Paul what could have happened to me. I told about
that pain and that I had felt really bad pain.

– I thought I had a heart attack and that I could die
from that pain, I explained to Paul worriedly. Paul
said with a smile that it was all because the spirit
had come near me, and I had not let the spirit into
me. I was really shocked, but I just thanked him
for the info.

I thought that if the approach of a spirit is like
that and hurts so much, how can it be a good spirit.
And if it's a good spirit, why does it hurt me.

I wanted a private session with Paul, which he
recommended if in doubt. He mentioned that he

could not guarantee a session for everyone, as time was limited. That caused a rush of appointment bookers to him.

I was also in line, and I was nervous about whether I would get a session to myself. Luck was on my side.

Paul was at peace when he contacted the spirits he used in these sessions. Then he began to speak.

– Let's look at you and see what you see, Paul began. – I get information from the spirit world. Then Paul said that he sees people in Finland from whom I have tried to hide my light, and that the last days he has seen my light, even though I was shy to show it at first.
– I have been contacting you for the past few days and I can see your light now. You are an extremely talented person; you have already worked with the spirit world. You can do anything as a medium, anything is possible, you have gifts.

Paul spoke slowly and convincingly. He was in a trance and his speech came directly from the spirit world.

– I haven't seen it before, but now in the last few days it has come up. Teaching is extremely important to you; you need to start teaching! You will be a great teacher, Paul continued. – I suggest a spiritual association, they are looking for students and tutors, so you can work from home. That would be a good start for you. I'm excited for you because I see where you are now, and I know you can go wherever you want. Your spiritual healing is really strong and your connection to the spirit world is really strong. Paul went on and on and I listened.

– You can give a lecture to people; you could do that more than anything else. Sessions are your thing, but you need more confidence. You have received more of it in the past few days.
Stage medium could be your thing; I can see you talking to people.
– I have indeed done that, I managed to interrupt.
– Don't set preconceptions in the sessions, for some reason you are afraid to show people what you know and what you do. I'm really excited for you. You can do sessions however you like, even with the help of Tarot cards.
– No, Tarot cards are not my thing, I interrupted.
– I do energy therapy and then at the end I talk about what I saw and experienced during the therapy. I see things symbolically, I told Paul.
– The next step is trance speech, because the best and most effective healers become trance speakers, Paul stated.
– The spirit world says to put the words to you. Then you don't say what the customer wants to hear, but what the spirit world says. You don't

even have to know what's being said, Paul said
with a smile.
– Has someone told you that you can't? Is that why
you hide your gifts? Paul asked. I didn't answer,
still listening as Paul continued:

– In trance, you are asleep, and you cannot analyze
what you say. Your gift as a teacher is shining
through now.
– I've run media circles, but that makes me feel
like the leader of the circle, and that's not right for
me, I was told in the meantime.
– Well, Finns, Paul laughed out loud – too modest.
– I encourage people, but I don't lie, Paul's tone
became serious.
– You have fantastic opportunities Ella, really
fantastic. You just have to trust the spirit world
and they will give you anything. You have to get
out of that doubting mindset and surrender, Paul
continued to speak in a serious and convincing
tone.
– Everything is easy for you, whatever you decide
to do. All your other therapies will improve
because the spirit world is involved. Customers get
more and more from your therapies. When you just
let go and give permission to the spirit world.
Paul's speech was impressive and made me believe
that he (or indeed the spirit world that spoke
through him) was serious.

– However, the most important thing is teaching.
You could teach a class here. Your spiritual
healing is really strong, and you could also be a
counselor. People would come to your reception
asking for advice and guidance, Paul listed.
– I already do something like that, a bit like by
accident, I said.
– There is no damage, Paul laughed. – You are so
creative, and you have opened up really well in the
last few days.
– I have done everything, I said. – I am in the
discomfort zone when I work as a medium, but
spiritual healing is my passion, I told Paul and
continued with the question:

– Another medium here told me in a session that
shamanism would be my thing, how does that fit
in?
– You can do anything like I said, try anything.
Whatever you do, you will succeed. You are very
talented, everything you do is successful. I hope
one day I see you in the next room teaching a
class. You have the competence to do all these, but
you need the first step, gather a group, teach it,
expand it, Paul guided and said that he sees a
beautiful energy around me. Paul mentioned that
he can see me teaching at this school.

– You could already teach, Ella, Paul assured and
continued: – You are already far ahead, and you
have talents. But if you want to proceed according

to the school's rules and get a teaching license in England, you are required to be trained as a spiritual healer.

My interest was immediately piqued. So, I could develop further and hardly many people would have that education in Finland.

I had always been looking for some purpose in my life without finding it. Maybe this would now be my life mission, which my soul had been thirsting for years.

I lived as if in a dream for a long time after the training and as soon as I got home, I sent a request to become a member of the organization Paul mentioned. That membership was needed so that I could study to become a Healer.

A little paperwork was required, but I got everything sent for membership.
After a couple of weeks of agony, I received an email about the approval, and the membership card and the first material would come in the mail.

I was looking forward to it and when that envelope with the Royal Mail stamp arrived, I was overjoyed.

The study would take place online as online teaching in the evenings, the material had to be read and the assignments done and sent to England for evaluation. The training would last two years. The answers to the assignments had to be long essays and the references had to be listed. The layout had to be exactly according to the instructions with paragraph divisions and line spacing. The minimum word count was set, and the source references had to be mentioned. The essay had to be original, but strictly based on the material. You got points for everything in the study notebook.

In England, vacancies on the website of the employment office sometimes ask for Healers for the terminal departments of hospitals. Maybe I could spend some time in England and try a job as a Healer. My thoughts were already flying in the future and far from reality.

The first online training was about to start, and I was looking forward to seeing our sympathetic teacher, Paul.

His face came out on the screen accurately and he greeted everyone. I immediately noticed nervousness in his being. He didn't smile, and he didn't talk nice.

– Well, this is official training, so maybe the rules are strict, I thought. But my mind was still reeling.

I felt that Paul was extremely stressed. Kindness was away and he was even clearly annoyed by the group's questions.

– Read your material before the online trainings, he said.

Paul previously said that he was giving up his very successful business or giving it to his wife. It surprised me, but I understood that Paul wanted to follow his heart or lead or whatever it was for him. Maybe he had some business-related problems or problems at home now. Usually, my instincts proved those feelings correct.

I had hardly been able to meditate before my trip to England, except for brief moments of yoga relaxation. Paul taught me that skill and I really thought that with the help of that meditation I could get to God. There was an insanely bright light, lots of light beings, angels of light and that wonderful feeling when you let go and "go with the flow".

Only later did I understand that those "presence" exercises where we were "absent" are precisely those moments when we let a certain power influence us.

It felt heavenly at first and when the teacher talked about light and God and assured me that he was telling the truth, why would I have questioned it. And even though I always doubted everything, like Paul's teachings at first, he got hold of me.

   And he had said that I could develop and teach,
so he saw potential in me. Or not just him, but the
spirit world. This would be my soul mission, and
God's will, I began to be quite sure of it.

The angels that I began to sense and see convinced
me even more. In no previous training had I sensed
angels so strongly. They really were present and
dazzled with their brightness. And I felt them, I
felt their presence and that feeling was real.
– In England they talked about God differently
than in Finland, that's the difference, I explained to
myself. This had to be what I've been looking for
all my life!

After my education in England, Finnish mediums
seemed to me to lose their importance. I thought
they did not take their work seriously and even
joked about it.

   I knew that a medium is either born or studied
and awareness opens with years of experience. In
Finland, that training was not respected at all, but
some of the mediums organized weekend courses,
on the basis of which one could start doing
sessions.

   In England, it was thought that this was quite
irresponsible, and in Finland, on the other hand,
there was a gloved reference to English strictness.
In England, supervision was strict regarding

studies, and in Finland anyone can teach or hold sessions, even if only based on a weekend course.

Now the going is even wilder; it seems that there are tens of mediums and clairvoyants in every city in Finland, and they have no training whatsoever.

I was enchanted by the English style of taking things seriously and it seemed to me the only right way.

Studying to become a Healer was not easy. Writing many strips of text took all my time.

When I finished and sent the essay, it was already time for the next on-line training, and I had to prepare for it by reading the assignments given the previous time.

A few times I already considered giving up, because the level of demand was so high. But something kept me going. Something pushed me forward.

The assessment was harsh; I thought I had answered an essay in the second section comprehensively, but the Assessor only gave a satisfactory grade. So, I had to try harder.

I didn't realize that I was doing all that at the extremes. I had my own job, family, my therapy job and now this study. The dark circles around my eyes told me how little sleep I had, when I wanted to develop with great passion.

Afterwards, I thought that I was "taken" and I didn't even understand what was wrong. I was in the grip of something bigger, but I didn't think about it at the time.

Then when the computer did the trick and the online connection failed, I started to panic. Someone now wanted to complicate my doings...

THIRTEEN

I also became interested in other spiritually awake influencers. My thirst for knowledge was endless.

I found a writer/healer who had experienced paranormal phenomena since childhood. His family was devastated by everything that had happened; chairs and beds were moving, things were breaking, etc. I'll call that person John now.

John was examined in hospitals and a program was also made about him for television. When John started studying at the boarding school, fellow students and teachers could witness the movement of beds, etc.

I really had to get John's books to read, and I found a few in the second-hand bookshop. One of those books was from 1975 and talked about John's supernatural experiences. I read the book halfway through and then stopped. I felt strange while reading and decided that I would continue

another day. I went to the kitchen to make dinner for my family. The oven and microwave clocks were both 9 minutes ahead.
– Has there been a power cut today? I asked my husband.
– I don't know, how so? my husband asked.
 – Well, when the oven and microwave clocks are both at the wrong time, I answered.
My husband came into the kitchen to look at those digital clocks.
– During a power cut, the clock doesn't move forward, does it? my husband asked rhetorically.
– Just look, I exclaimed. – This must be Jaakko's jokes, I laughed and walked into my son's room.
– Jaakko, have you touched the clocks of the oven and microwave? I asked.
– Well, I don't! he replied without looking up from his cell phone.
– Hello, really, are you?
– What, I'm not, Jaakko answered a little annoyed.
– Why would I be? he asked.
I explained that both clocks advance 9 minutes.
– Oh, he answered. It didn't interest him, but I did.
My husband claimed that I had inadvertently touched them, but I really hadn't. He set the clocks to the right time, we ate dinner and went to bed.

When I woke up in the morning, both clocks were ahead again. 11 minutes now. – It can't be true, I thought to myself. The others had already left for work and school, so I was left alone to think. I was sure that reading that book moved those clocks.

I decided to contact the author of the book, John. I easily found his contact information and sent him a message via Facebook Messenger telling him how the times had changed while reading his book.

I browsed his pages and noticed that he was still organizing spiritual healing circles and courses. I was very interested in them and in my thoughts, I was already in England again.

When I sent a message to John, I was sure he wouldn't have the time or inclination to respond to that message, but he did, and even the same day. He thanked me for my message and told me that many have experienced similar things when reading his books, and that book in particular. He mentioned about the events in the book that the energy was still quite uncontrollable, when he was a child.

I was excited, secretly proud that he had answered me. I took that as a clear sign that I needed to meet him.

I started planning a trip to England to his healing circle. He organized them all over England and they seemed to be popular. I chatted with him and asked about those courses. However, arranging the times was difficult. I didn't have any extra vacation days left.

Even though John seemed like an extremely interesting person and was sympathetic, I still decided not to finish reading that book of his, even the cover picture was kind of scary. I threw the book in the trash.

I was going deeper and deeper into spirituality and nothing seemed to be enough. I had to get more of all this, I had to experience more deeply, reach higher vibrations.

My hunger for spirituality seemed endless. Sometimes I felt like it wasn't enough, but something made me push forward even harder.

My husband also interfered sometimes, and then I felt very guilty that I was "away" so much. Even though I was at home, I was completely absent, because I was either doing study assignments or something related to spirituality. Giving energy therapies and helping clients voluntarily, also by phone and email, took their own time, and there were many people who requested it. I did a lot of work without compensation.

I wanted to help as many as possible, but it came at a price.

My son started to crave time together and I didn't seem to have time. All that time I spent helping others was away from my family who missed me.

I felt an inner compulsion to do this helping work, because it was "God's work."

FOURTEEN

I prayed every night and morning. I had been doing that for years and it felt right to me. And the knowledge that this spirituality was not at odds with God felt comforting. That's what I was told, and I helped people from my heart.

I started to gather a group to whom I could pass on that loving distance healing, and there were plenty of willing people. Once a month I channeled loving healing energy for 20 minutes. The recipients felt from tingling to quite strong physical sensations.

Mediums came to Finland from England, and I wanted to attend their courses.

One of my spiritual (New Age) friends praised an English long-line psychic medium who was coming to Finland just during my vacation.

I was ready to sign up for the course, because I knew that English mediums were in a completely different compared to Finnish ones. They were more serious and committed and learned.

In that course we did a trance mediumship where we met our deceased loved ones. It was a wonderful feeling when I saw, heard and felt the mother who came to meet and greet me during those trance exercises. I seriously thought it was my late mother; it looked the same, felt the same and talked the same. I couldn't imagine that some spirit could pretend to be my mother. (Ironic, because I should have understood that the spirit world is capable of all kinds of things). I didn't see my father; I only felt him from afar. Instead, I felt a large metallic angel close behind me as I tried to connect with father. That angel was powerful, and it was bigger than the room.

I learned to ask advice from the deceased about things that had remained secrets in my family. I got answers and even names, which I then wrote down and decided based on them to start researching the roots of my family. But that had to wait, because I had other things to do now.

That English psychic medium held another medium event in the evening, which I participated in. The medium said at first that a lady from the spirit world had been in the space we were in all day. He described the lady and her character, and I recognized my mother immediately.

– This lady has been here since morning and has been shouting that she wants me to tell her daughter that her mother is present, the medium laughed. I knew that mom would be just that impatient. Big tears came to my eyes, and I started to cry a lot. I missed my mother very much, even though it had already been six years since she died. This all deepened the feeling that I want to continue this path. I wanted to go back to England to develop more. I wasn't interested in any Finnish doctrine anymore, because it wasn't disciplined and regular, not very deep either.

I met new clients and my abilities continued to develop.

Then I attended a popular medium fair where a medium was talking about different medium abilities, and I discovered that I had them all.
I felt like that medium was talking to me. Everything she said seemed to hit the nail on the head. I nodded my head as she spoke. I stated that I was clairaudient, clairvoyant, clairvoyant, I sensed mental states and had premonitions.
So, I had been directed to this fair so that I could hear that and be convinced of it. This was guidance from above, it had now been shown to me.

I was excited and happy about it all, but I was careful not to become boastful, because I knew it would lead in another direction.

It was a gift or gifts and I had learned that they had to be developed and used, otherwise they would be lost. And that was said to be absolute, they would certainly be lost if they were not adopted and developed.

FIFTEEN

My reputation as a seer, medium and helper had grown and once while sitting in my office at work I heard cries for help.

– Help, help, help, someone shouted. That sounded like it was coming from somewhere far away and I quickly ran to another room where my colleagues were sitting having coffee.
– Did you hear someone calling for help somewhere? I asked alarmed. My colleagues seemed puzzled and worried.
– I didn't hear anything, replied Liisa.
– Neither do I, said Sirkka.
– I heard, for sure, I said. They were still looking at me a little surprised.
– Am I going crazy, I laughed, but I knew I heard the cries for help. Just then my phone started ringing.

– Hello, answered the gentle woman's voice and continued:
– Could you help me? I've been thinking about calling you for a long time when you've been recommended, but I haven't, the female voice continued to speak.

I was dumbfounded. I mean, did I hear the hallways, first I hear a cry for help and then someone calls and asks for help. This was a clear sign for me that I must now help. The woman introduced herself as Tarja. He said that she had contracted cancer and received harsh and extremely tiring cytostatic therapies. Tarja couldn't come to my therapy room, so she asked me for distance energy therapy. I promised Tarja that I could visit her home for therapy.

I went to Tarja the following Sunday and told her about Healing. Tarja wanted to receive that, even though she didn't know what it actually was.

– It feels good, Tarja said when I started treating her.

I visited Tarja every two weeks throughout that summer and it seemed to be the highlight of Tarja's life. She was lonely and her only sister was very busy.

SIXTEEN

My former neighbor Paavo had always believed in God, even though his wife Aili was an atheist.

They were like night and day, but Paavo adored his wife until she died. Paavo was kind and Aili was demanding.

This couple had been my neighbors for five years when their son Harry, who is in his thirties, returned home from the world. He had pursued an IT career in Sweden and then left for India. No one ever mentioned what he was doing in India, and I didn't ask.

Paavo had his hands full with Aili, whose health had failed, so the boy's help was welcome. I didn't know their son Harry before, but I soon realized that he was more like his mother than his father.

Aili's condition worsened and she wanted to be at home until the end.

One night in November, Aili then moved from time to eternity. Or did she...

After that, in December, I was at a charity sale, where all literature related to esotericism and New Age, crystals, etc. were sold.

I bumped into Harry at the store and was very surprised, and his expression told that the surprise was mutual.

– Oh, you're also interested in these things, Harry asked.
– Yes, and actually a little bit more, I answered, and a great feeling of pride went through me.
– Please tell me more, Harry got excited.
– Well, I am e.g. a medium, I said almost in a whisper.
– Really? Harry's face tightened.
– I'm sorry about your mother's passing, I said and touched Harry's upper arm. Harry flinched and thanked me.
I apologized to Harry that I had to leave. I had promised to do a medium session for a lady.

As I drove up to that lady, I felt a small twinge of conscience in my chest. Why had I told Harry about my medium abilities.

The year changed and I saw Paavo more often outside working in the snow. I had already taken my condolences to him in November and around Christmas I took a Christmas flower. He was very broken, and I tried my best to comfort him.

Now he was somehow feeling tired.

– Hey, how are you, I shouted from behind the fence. Paavo came to the fence and said he was very tired. He was kind of reserved.
– Yes, it will ease, he said, turning to continue making snow.

I was left thinking about Paavo. Something wasn't right now, I sensed something different in him. And Harry's interest in New Age was still confusing to me. I had met many people, but Harry was not the type of "spiritual" person at all. Well, maybe I'm overthinking and overanalyzing.
The answer to my thoughts came pretty soon when I met Harry near the mailbox the next day. He said he wanted to talk to me, and I asked him for tea.

Over that cup of tea, he surprised me even more.

– Aili is back, he began. I had just sipped some
peppermint tea and now it was about to come out
of my mouth as I gasped in shock.
– What do you mean, Harry, I slurred.
– Just one evening, father fell into a deep state and
said that mother is here, Harry said and continued
enthusiastically: – Mother has told me now things
that only she can know. She also told how she
wants to be buried and what kind of funeral she
wants.

I couldn't believe my ears. So, this is happening to
me now, can this even happen.

Harry spoke enthusiastically about the "channel"
that mother and father had formed.

– Does Aili talk to you? I asked.
– She speaks, but only through father, Harry
answered determinedly.

Harry left and I told him that I would be happy to
talk to Paavo about it if he was ready for it. Harry
promised to get back to it.

I haven't been seen Harry and Paavo for many
weeks and I was worrying if something had
happened.

One Sunday evening, I saw Paavo in his garden and waved to say hello. Paavo waved back and asked me to the fence.

– Can you come inside? he asked timidly.
– Oh, of course, I answered without hesitation.

Harry was not at home and Paavo asked me to sit in the kitchen. I suddenly felt a cold breeze pass me. The feeling was unpleasant, but I sensed that it was some spirit.

– Harry has already told you about this channel, Paavo began.
– Yes, I answered as if it were every day for me. Paavo told how everything had started quite suddenly after Aili's death. He explained that he fell into a sleep-like state with a loud noise.

– Just like having the wrong station on the radio, you know? he asked. I nodded; I knew that was a normal sound in these contexts.
– After all, this is very comforting that we got Aili back like this as a miracle of God, Paavo said and sighed.
– Yes, I said and found myself hesitating. I wondered about my own behavior and the question that came to my mind as if someone had told me: God? I was irritated by my own thought, where did such a question come to my mind.

– Is something wrong? I asked.
– Yes and no, Paavo said with concern on his face.
– This communication is extremely exhausting, I don't want to take it at all, Paavo sighed and continued:
– I must go to sleep as soon as the channel closes.
– How long is that channel open at a time and can you regulate it? I asked.

Paavo said that the channel is open for up to an hour every day and that it takes away his strength. I advised him to take a break from that contact, because I knew from experience how even just one session drains a younger person's strength. At that time, I felt as if the kitchen ceiling had caved in. I felt a heavy energy on my shoulders. Paavo didn't seem to notice or sense that at all.

– That is not under my control, Paavo said sadly.

I told him how the medium must draw the line between when the spirit can come and when not. That's what I was taught. Again, the energy weighed on my shoulders. I tried to straighten my back and find a better position. Paavo said that no matter how hard he tried, it didn't work. I asked Paavo to practice that.

– It is so comforting when Aili is still here and we can talk, Paavo smiled.

– I guess I can handle this. I don't want to bother you with these troubles, but thank you for your time, Paavo said, and I knew he wanted me to leave.
At the front door, Paavo panicked, because Harry was just coming in.

– Oh, you here, Harry was surprised, and I sensed his irritation.
– Ella gave some practical advice, Paavo laughed forcefully.

At home, I wondered how Paavo had become a medium in just one night. Was the spirit world so powerful that it can contact and demand contact. That's not how it should be according to anything I've learned. I was in awe, and on the other hand, the thought seemed scary.

Time passed again and I didn't catch a glimpse of Paavo or Harry. I was on a business trip myself and on vacation with my family.

There was less and less time left for the family because of all the media sessions, trainings and courses. I also had to take care of work and home. Something had to change, it couldn't go on like this. My family clearly suffered.

My 10-year-old son had nightmares and started talking about how he felt like there were others in our house at night. I cleaned our house with sage when I was alone at home, I clapped my hands in the corners and conjured to remove evil spirits.

Then I saw Harry at the end of the summer cutting the fence and I decided to go talk. We talked about this, and I sensed that Harry wanted to avoid me somehow.

I cautiously asked if Aili was still "present".

– Yes, strongly! Harry nudged almost unkindly.
– Okay, how is Paavo, he hasn't been seen? I asked again.
– Very well, Harry said and continued to cut the fence.
– Well, say greetings from me, I blurted out. Harry didn't answer.

I guessed that Harri didn't want me to have anything to do with Paavo. Well, what am I to interfere in their affairs. I left them alone until one autumn evening Paavo came behind the door.
– Is everything okay? I asked.
– I need to talk, is that okay now? Paavo sounded a little alarmed.
I asked Paavo to come in and made some tea. The rest of my family was busy with their hobbies, and I always had time if someone needed help.

– I have thought about whether this is right. Has God sent Aili to me? Paavo said quietly.
– You want my opinion, don't you? I asked.
Paavo nodded.
– I think Aili is in an intermediate state and is not in heaven. She should be guided to the light so that she can find peace, I told Paavo.
– How is she not in the light? Paavo was confused.

I told Paavo what I had learned. I said that the wandering spirits should be guided to the light.
– I thought you were a medium, Paavo was amazed.
– Well, but this is how it should go, I argued.

I was so unsure of what I said because my mind was screaming believe me now: It's not Aili!

– Well, thanks for the tea, but I guess I must leave, Paavo said and sipped his tea.

He left and I was left to settle myself. Why couldn't I tell him. I was pretty confused about everything that happened to me. I decided to give myself time.

I planned a lot in my mind about everything related to mediumship and spiritual healing.

I would hold trainings, spiritual healing circles, I could make trips to see John, for example, etc.

I started to prepare a spiritual healing course; I had already given one to a few people I trusted.

Paul had said that it didn't have to be what he taught, but that we could change it as we pleased.

I had changed the training in such a way that I first asked for the Holy Spirit, because I thought it was right.

On the other hand, I had also started to think about what the purpose of all this spirituality was and what was its origin. Was this really all from God?

I had read medium manuals and several English-language articles about the birth of spiritualism, waded through numerous articles on the subject on the internet and bought old books on the subject from old bookstores, but something seemed to be missing or something didn't match. Everything didn't feel right.

It was the eighth of August and the astrological Leo Gate Day. I was alone at home and suddenly I was overcome by a wild uncertainty.

Was I on the right path?

I was walking from room to room, restless and feeling strange. What on earth is bothering me, I can't rest from this thought.

Is this right, something is wrong, who can tell me… I was getting desperate.

Where did all these questions come from and where did this feeling come from, which was getting stronger all the time, and which had been in the background for some time.

I felt like screaming. My feeling became more and more unbearable, and I went from room to room in a panic. I started to feel pain and it was hard to breathe. What exactly is this?

I decided to pray.

– God, is this right, am I on the right path, I
prayed.
– God, can you hear me? I prayed quietly at first
and then in a louder voice.

I was already on the verge of despair, because I
needed an answer. I felt awful. I started crying and
calling out to God. I clenched my crossed hands
tightly and was full of pain.

– God, dear God, is this right, I cried and
screamed.

At the same time, I felt how strong, a "voiceless"
voice said: "WHAT DO YOU BELIEVE".
That voice could be heard from the walls and the
ceiling and everywhere, it was so strong that it was
everywhere at the same time. It's hard to explain
that in words. I knew immediately that God was
speaking to me.

He answered!!

That sound made me drop to my knees and raise
my praying hands. I cried aloud and shouted:

– In God, I believe in God!! I was on my knees
crying, crying out to God and testifying my faith in
Him. It felt like the only right thing for me to do.

At the same time, an incredible feeling of peace came over me.

– Now I know, I said out loud and continued to cry. Now my crying was different, I was infinitely grateful, and it made me cry as well.

Next, I was directed to look up certain verses in the Bible. My grandmother's Bible, which had seen life, was on the bookshelf in my bedroom, and I hurried to get my hands on it. The Bible in question is from 1933, so its wording differs slightly from the latest translation of the Bible.

I didn't know the Bible, because I had never read it. Now I knew what to look for, it was pointed out to me. The book of Moses was quickly found. The exact scripture that was pointed out to me was Leviticus 19:31:

"Do not turn to mediums or seek out spiritists, for you will be defiled by them. I am the Lord your God."

And I was shown yet another passage from Deuteronomy 18:10–13, which says:

"Let no one be found among you who sacrifices their son or daughter in the fire, who practices divination or sorcery, interprets omens, engages in witchcraft, or casts spells, or who is a medium or spiritist or who consults the dead. Anyone who does these things is detestable to the Lord; because of these same detestable practices the Lord your God will drive out those nations before you. You must be blameless before the Lord your God."

I had done all that and it was against God's will.

– What have I done! I held my head in my hands and felt guilty.

That guilt felt gnawing and made me scream.

– No! I shouted crying. I fell to my knees again, now of my own accord, and my crying continued.

Guilt is a terrible burden. I felt it now to the core of my heart.

God made me question everything I saw, felt, did in my sleep and awake. I screamed and cried again.

– I don't do anything that is against God's will! – I don't do it, and I don't want to, I shouted even more guilty.

Then a huge amount of anger and strength gathered in me, and I told everything else to go away.

– Disappear everything that is not from God, I shouted furiously. – Get out, get out, I shouted louder and louder.

I felt cleansed. Then I prayed, thanked God and felt relief.

I felt great gratitude that I had now been given that feeling and question and had received a clear answer to it.

The things I did were not for God, but against Him. Acting as a medium had never felt good or even like my thing, if I was honest with myself.

I destroyed with great fury by tearing up and burning all the literature related to message transmission and I also destroyed the materials of the basic medial course.

It felt good to get rid of all that material against God's will.

I had already left that Finnish spiritualistic society before, because Leila had threatened and pressured me.

I began to pray that my neighbor Aili would rest and that the Lord would lead her husband Paavo and his son Harry to the truth. I didn't know if they wanted it, so I was a little careful with my prayers.

EIGHTEEN

Then in the fall I saw Paavo raking and waved my hand to say hello.

– Hello, shouted Paavo briskly and walked quickly towards me.
– Wait, I have something for you, he whimpered. I left the keys in the front door and stepped to the fence.
– Something is happening now, Paavo began. He blinked around as if afraid of something.
– Aili is moving dishes, Paavo said. – And spice jars, he continued.
– She is dissatisfied with the order I made in the kitchen, and she tells me in communication how to do and organize everything as before, Paavo spoke quickly and was a bit excited.
– This is heavy, but I'll do it when I'm asked from heaven to do so, Paavo said thoughtfully.

– Oh no, I thought. How would you put this into words so as not to offend.

I was just about to say something "wise" when Paavo continued: – I've already come twice to ring your doorbell to talk about these things with you, but something has always happened that I haven't been able to make it.

My interest was piqued, because I felt that the spirit did not want Paavo to meet me.

– So what? I asked.
– Well, the smoke alarm started going off, even though there were no carts anywhere. I searched and examined every device, but everything was as it should be. In the end, I changed the battery in the fire alarm and decided to stay and observe the situation. Another time there was a pile of small stones on the hall floor, and I slipped on them. My knee hurt excruciatingly, and I couldn't move properly for a couple of days. I also asked Harry about the stones, but he didn't know anything about them. We wondered together how they had appeared there, Paavo said, rubbing his chin.

I did know what it was about; the spirit did not want us to meet.

Paavo and Harry didn't stop to chat after that, they just greeted from afar. They always seemed to be in a hurry if I tried to get a conversation going.

Then one day they had just moved out with saying goodbye. My other neighbor told me about it. I was confused and a little sad.

I went through a hard struggle inside when I went to meet Tarja. Everything I did was questioned by God.

I had talked to Tarja about energies and other things after death, and now I had been shown that they were illusions, and my faith in them was beginning to waver.

– Whatever happened, I thought, but I'm going to Tarja's. I was going to tell the truth.

– Tarja, I was "spoken to" and I feel that God spoke to me. I don't want to talk anymore about energies or the spirit world, I said cautiously. – I'm sorry if this seems confusing to you, but I feel like I'm finding the truth. I believe in God and always have, I continued.
– Yes, everything you have done has been a great help, Tarja said. – It saddens me that I can't compensate you in any way, because I don't have any money, she said, pressing her head.
– I don't want money from you Tarja, I got a request to help you, I got the sign I told you about earlier, I assured her.

– If you can, I would still like that Healing, Tarja said.
– Of course, but I'll do it in a different way now, praying, is that okay? I asked.

I had thought in my mind that if I do spiritual healing by praying, it would not be against God's will.
– That's fine, said Tarja.

Then one fall Sunday when I went to see Tarja, she seemed hopeless.

– My chemotherapy is now finished, now they just focus on treating the pain, she said quietly. I gritted my teeth so I wouldn't burst into tears. I knew what this meant and tried to pull myself together.

– Oh Tarja, I said and hugged her.

Despite everything, Tarja wanted to receive Healing and I continued it every couple of weeks by visiting her to give it.

Then a message came from Tarja that she had been transferred to the hospital for hospice care. I went to see Tarja every week and she told me that another woman also visited her as a volunteer. Tarja mentioned that woman by name and I recognized her.

Eija was deep in New Age and constantly trained to increase her skills. I didn't know that she also did volunteer work for hospice patients, so I was surprised when I heard about this from Tarja, but I tried to hide my surprise.

Tarja said that Eija's visits do not feel good and right, and she does not want Eija to come anymore.

I prayed the Our Father prayer to Tarja when I couldn't do anything else, even though Tarja wasn't interested in religious matters in any way. She was very thankful for the prayer.

After that, I always took the New Testament with me and read verses from it to her. In Tarja's opinion, listening to those verses felt good. She was very tired and exhausted.
She would always fall asleep before I finished reading, then I would cover her and hold her hand.

One time she opened her eyes when I touched her hand. She tried to say hello but was too tired to say anything.

– Hey, hey, just sleep. See you again, I told her with a smile.
When I left at that time, I decided that in a few days I would go again, she was so weak. After getting on the bus, tears came to my eyes. I couldn't stop the tears that broke out. People turned

to look, but I didn't care about their looks. I knew in my heart that was the last time I would see Tarja.

I didn't make it to Tarja anymore when her sister sent me a sad message that Tarja had passed away.

Tarja's death caused me great sadness, I cried inconsolably like a small child gasping for breath. I knew I was crying for all my other losses too – once again. I had swept the grief of my brother's and mother's deaths under the rug, because mediums don't grieve. They always have a connection with the departed, and thus there is no death.
Now all that was a slap the face. The grief caused by death was real and final.

All this was exhausting me. I felt helpless in the face of death.

I decided that I will refrain from voluntary hospice care from now on.
I felt powerless and sad that I couldn't help. I had imagined that spiritual healing or combining it with prayer would help.

NINETEEN

Mari, who was in England at the same time as me, frequently attended various courses and sessions.

I had gotten to know her in the basic mediumship course and right from the start she seemed like such a natural and nice friend. She was somehow uncomplicated and approachable.

Mari did various therapies guided by helpers from the spirit world. Almost every time we talked, she talked about the new helper and the helper's abilities.

Mari had great sorrows behind her. Her teenage daughter had taken her own life a few years ago.

We met by chance over there in England and found ourselves on the same Healing course.

Mari spent hours every day doing those meditations we learned, so she "progressed" faster. Sometimes I felt like I couldn't understand if she was talking about real people or spirits from the spirit world. For her they were all every day present and they controlled what she did.

I was worried about it, but I didn't realize at the time that I too was fast approaching the same situation.

Our teacher Paul was coming to Finland later that year and Mari was excited about it. I was not able to tell Mari that I am no longer interested in the subject, because I had been shown in August that I was on the wrong path. However, I said yes when she asked if I would attend the course and go together.

I had already decided to stop my studies in the English spiritual community, but I hadn't resigned yet. I didn't want to get into a situation where our teacher arriving in Finland would ask me for reasons.
During that course, I also met other wonderful people who were in England. Our teacher was kind, and we went through much the same things as in England.

– He is not a psychic medium, but feels different, I thought. Then I would encourage my mind and ask where does this power come from that we connect with?
– From God, Ella. Don't you remember I already told you that in England, Paul replied with a friendly smile and continued:
– When you do Healing, you are connected to a pure source, not anywhere else.

His being was completely different now than I remembered it being in the online education. Paul was now relaxed and smiling a lot. There was something good about him. – He's probably the only one in that whole school who really believes in God, I thought.

Maybe I could continue Healing even if I quit all messaging from spirit world. Healing cannot be contrary to God's will!

During the course, Paul convinced me that this knowledge from God could and should be shared.

That skill he had taught us was meant to be shared so that we could change the world for the better.

– Everyone can modify it in their own way.

– Do you want to be changing the world? he asked
a few times, and I answered in my mind:
– Yes, I am going to share this information with
others as well. Yes, I want to change the world.

On the way home, my thoughts were already
flying into the future, and I had decided to hold a
few courses on the subject for people and continue
to do free distance Healing.

After that happening in August, I had already
done distance Healing so that I was praying the
whole time, not just "floating".

I also often prayed to Jesus, and it always brought
tears to my eyes. At the end of the session, I
always cried profusely.

– Mother, I cried in pain and cried. I had lost my
mother; my mother was dead, and I cried
inconsolably and called out to her. I knew I was
going to scream, and I winced and then woke up. I
was scared. I was completely silent. My husband
had also woken up to my painful screams. In that
dream, I lost my mother again.

She had already died 5 years ago and now I
experienced the pain of that loss again in a dream.
I already knew what that meant last night.

I soon went back to sleep, and my mother was in my dream again. She was sitting on a school bench in a big classroom waiting for me. But I always had something else to do and I didn't go to mom even though she was waiting. I didn't feel bad about letting her wait.

In the morning, I knew that this was another temptation of the spirit world to turn me back to mediumship. I had experienced the mother's presence and even talked to the mother last year while practicing trance mediumship. Mother came to me at that time, and she was happy. I was happy too to meet her and to be able to talk to her. It was wonderful and infinitely fascinating in its own way. It also increased my self-esteem when I was able to do that. I was clever, I was told.
I heard, saw and felt spirit world and I was extremely sensitive to all that.

Of course I miss my mother, I really do. I lost her far too soon, I would have needed my mother's advice on many more things, but I would no longer contact the spirits of the deceased.

I knew that dream was showing me how I would lose mom again and again when I didn't keep in touch with her. And that dream also showed me that my mother is waiting for me at school (medium school) which I left behind me.

TWENTY

Mari had decided to go to another medium session and lecture. I wondered about her activity and how her money was enough for all that. On the other hand, I knew it was hard for her to say no, and I understood that she wanted to receive messages from her daughter.

Leila was organizing that event and a psychic medium named Juhani had been invited.

Juhani had said in that lecture that he was in contact with semi-angels and said that they were the highest vibrating beings that exist. During the lecture, someone made the mistake of asking if Jesus is not the highest. Juhani had almost thrown up when he heard the word Jesus, and the people present were quite amazed.

Juhani is self-confident, persuasive and a good speaker, he easily draws the listener in and he also has a certain kind of charisma.

After the lecture, he had given private sessions for a fee, and Mari had wanted to participate in one as well.

Juhani had told Mari, for example, that she had bad karma from her parents and that it should be removed. Karma removal could be done over the phone and a few phone conversations were needed. The price for that karma removal would be 400 euros. Mari was hesitant to buy that, because her financial situation was bad after the renovation of the apartment. However, Juhani had assured that Mari needed that course to move forward in her life. He had also given Mari some codes.

When Mari called me and told me all that, I got angry for her. I often knew scammers or "other side actors" based on their voice or story alone, and this felt exactly like that. I didn't hide my feelings and my horror at all when I asked Mari that if she didn't already notice Juhani's reaction to the word of Jesus!
– That is clearly on the evil side, and not just unknowingly but quite consciously, I was shocked at my words.

– And those codes! They are not used by the good spirit world! I shouted to Mari on the phone.
– I thought so little too, Mari answered quietly. She feared my reaction and was a little hurt.

– Sorry, I didn't mean to offend, but dear Mari, I SEE what that man is!! It's best for you to forget the whole thing now, I said calmly, even though my heart was beating really hard, as it always does when I feel that someone has faced injustice.
– I already ordered that karma removal, Mari said timidly.
– Cancel it right away, I said demandingly. I don't tend to be demanding, but when I feel and feel that someone is being abused, it's hard for me to control my agitation.

I heard from Mari's voice that she was scared even by the thought of calling the man and canceling the deal. I offer to call for Mari, but Mari said she would call herself. I asked Mari to call me immediately after the phone conversation.

A few days passed and then Mari called.

Juhani had sounded angry and tried to make Mari change her mind even more. However, Mari had remained firm, and had the deal been cancelled, she wouldn't have had the money for that. Mari had immediately felt bad energy during the call.

– It was a really good decision that you called and canceled that Mari, I said from my heart, because I knew it was in Mari's best interest.

Spirituality teaches that one should not interfere in another's path, but I did so because I cared about my friend, who was clearly being led in the wrong direction.

At that moment I still didn't know what was to come.

A few days later, Mari called me in a panic.

– They won't leave me alone, Mari said in distress.
– Which ones, Mari, which ones? I asked.
– I haven't been able to sleep, because they keep me awake. They come from my legs to my body and won't go away. Mari sounded confused and at first, I thought she was having a seizure.
– Are you alone, do you need an ambulance? I asked.
– No, nothing like that. Those codes have been activated; I know... Mari was silent after that. It was difficult for me to find out what it was all about, but it worked out when I calmed Mari down and asked her questions calmly. The codes given by that psychic medium, Juhani, had been activated and Mari started talking about them.

– No, don't talk, and don't say them out loud, I warned.

I didn't want to take the risk that I would get the curse too or that they would become stronger in Mari. What I did next was a guidance. I act by some greater power.

– Do you have a cross pendant, Mari? I asked.
– Yes, it's in a box somewhere.
– Take it out immediately and put it around your neck. Mari did the work as ordered. She had found another cross as well and held it in her hands.

I felt Mari's pain and felt the evil power even on the phone. I kept praying to God and Jesus in my mind.

I knew that I got the strength and wisdom to do things by doing that.

– They don't like this, Mari said quietly.
– You are stronger than them, I said. Mari started to cry.
– Do you have a Bible, I asked.
– Yes, Mari said.
– Take it in your hand, I instructed.
– It feels better, Mari said.
– Do not be afraid. Pray, Mari! Ask Jesus Christ to protect you. I wondered about my speech; it was new to me.

We had been talking for another hour and it was getting late. Mari said that she would dare to sleep.

– Yes, you dare, I said. – Keep the Bible close to you, and you'll fall asleep, good night.

When I went to sleep that night, I prayed many times and asked Mari for blessing and protection. I didn't know what else to say. My husband wondered about the content of the call as he heard some parts of it. I knew if I told him he would think I was crazy. This sounded incredible to me, like something from the movie The Exorcist, but I knew it was all true. Mari was not crazy, deranged or mentally ill.

After a couple of days, I called Mari again. She said that the crosses and the Bible helped and that she felt pretty good.

– Yes, the cross has a wonderful and powerful energy, she stated. – When I hold them in my hands, they literally tingle, Mari continued.

The next day, Mari had read the spiritual society's publication, and with that, the evil spirits had returned to the place. She had woken up in the night to find that those spirits were in her again.

The Bible had fallen to the floor, and she had stayed awake for the rest of the night.

Mari said that minor spirits disappear with the help of the cross and the Bible, but while sleeping, higher level spirits come and take contact. Spirits tormented her awake and asleep.

I promised to pray for her and do Healing for her and call the next day.

I did a distance Healing for Mari, at the end I opened the New Testament and it opened with a passage that says: "repent and let each one of you be baptized in the name of Jesus Christ for the forgiveness of your sins, and you will receive the gift of the Holy Spirit." I also read chapters from the Gospel of Luke and the Gospel of Moses.

Mari said that it had started happening right away. The evil had escaped, but it had remained spinning.

– It doesn't know whether to leave or come back, Mari explained.
– Open the door and say out loud: I choose Jesus Christ, the rest can leave, I advised Mari.

I was no expert, but something told me to do it.

I thought to myself that this is guidance, God's guidance.

After we had discussed the matter again for several hours, I suggested that Mari ask Paul about it. Somehow, I still trusted him.

Mari called again a few days later.

– Paul couldn't help, she said sounding broken.
– He gave me distance Healing, but that doesn't help either, at first it seemed to help, but in the end it didn't, Mari wailed. Mari also asked me for Healing, and I promised to take care. I also said I would pray.

– Mari, promise me that you won't meditate, and you won't be in contact with the spirit world, I said in a strict tone of voice. I explained to Mari that it might increase that phenomenon. She was clearly possessed by the spirits and was unable to resist them.

  I prayed nonstop myself, because I knew that this was true, not a joke.
I asked Mary to pray.

– I have prayed and tried everything, she said clearly tired. Mari asked me to her place, but I couldn't travel because of work.

I searched for information about exorcisms on the pages of the Evangelical Lutheran Church without success. I found some old article on the Internet where a priest said that he had cast out evil spirits from women from Africa who said they were cursed. The whole topic seemed to be strange and unknown in the Evangelical Lutheran Church.

When Mari first called me about it, I told her to go to church. The churches were all closed at that time, but she had driven into the yard of a chapel and felt better there. But that torment returned as soon as she returned to her home.

I felt that I was being guided and what had happened to me that August day was a clear sign that I was not on the right path. However, I didn't know what else I could do for Mari, because I did believe in God, but I wasn't in faith and my knowledge of the Bible was quite poor.

I still imagined that the good spirit world, Helpers and spiritual Healing were from God and the evil one from the Devil. And I wanted to be on the good side, like most of the spiritual people I know.

I felt obliged to help my friend in every way, although I did not yet fully know how.

I browsed the Internet all night long and finally found a mention that the Catholic Church has an exorcist in Finland. The article I found didn't mention the name of that exorcist, but I decided to talk to Mari about it.
– I found out that the Catholic Church does exorcisms for real, and not just in movies, I told Mari.
– Oh, really? Mari answered hopefully.
– But unfortunately, I don't know that priest's name, I confessed.
– I know a Catholic woman, Mari said. – If I ask her.
– Do that, I said.

Mari told how more and more spirits are passing through her at night. And they wouldn't let her sleep.

– They use me all the time, Mari said.
– You must be strong and deny it, I advised Mari.
– They don't believe it, this is just a torture, Mari complained in despair and tiredness.

I had advised Mari to pray to God, Jesus and the Holy Spirit.

– Have you prayed Mari? I asked.
– Yes, I am, but I don't know if it will help. I no longer know what is true and what is not, Mari said.

Mari said that some spirits are really strong and when she had prayed, a really strong spirit had come to her and said it was Jesus. In the end, it had been something else entirely.

– How can I even trust prayer anymore; Mari was in pain.
– Don't give up Mari, promise you won't give up, I panicked.

A few days passed again. I thought of Mari every moment and prayed. I also tried that exorcism used by the Catholic Church myself: "In the name of Jesus Christ, get out of her."

But I thought I was not entitled to use it, so I decided to leave it to those ordained to the priesthood, if one should ever be found.

When we talked with Mari, she said that she had been to a Catholic mass, and it felt good. At home, however, everything returned.

She had discarded objects she had collected that seemed to have bad energy. I advised her to do so. Mari asked an evangelical Lutheran priest to bless her home and it had also felt good, until those spirits returned that same evening.

I haven't heard Mari for some time, and I felt quite tired and exhausted myself. What wore me out the most was not being able to help. I racked my brains over what I did wrong, but I couldn't figure it out.

When I finally got a message from Mari, it was from the hospital. Mari had asked for help from her friend, who was some kind of energy and Reiki healer.

A friend had wanted to help, but the Reiki therapy had "gone too far", as Mari expressed it. The friend had to order an ambulance and Mari was taken to the hospital, where she spent a few days under observation. Mari called me and whispered about it.

– Something powerful went through me and somehow, I went into a very strange state or lost consciousness. Another spirit left me, but a stronger one took its place, Mari whispered.

She said that all the words, and even the mere thoughts that referred to spirits, caused a strong upsurge of energies in the body. I felt a lot of pain, because I knew that treating with energies was the last thing that could be done in that state, but of course everyone meant well and tried to help.

The hospital found that Mari is not psychotic.

– I can't tell them what's really going on, because I would end up in a closed ward, Mari continued to whisper.

– This is like a movie, I said.

– Well, that's right, Mari stated. In the hospital, Mari was given strong sedatives, which helped her sleep.

She was also recommended for psychotherapy because of her past.

Mari had also told her Catholic friend about it, who had also prayed diligently for Mari.

Mari got home and stayed on a long sick leave. She went to Catholic Mass regularly, and she said it feels good.

That Catholic friend of Mari had arranged her an appointment with Catholic Psychotherapist. That Psychotherapist promised Mari to arrange a meeting with a Catholic priest. It all sounded right to me now, if only Mari could finally get out of this torment.

We spoke on the phone when Mari came from meeting that Catholic priest. Mari explained that she will go to that church in a week and the priest will read some text to her.

The priest had said that I could pray and join in, because the prayer he reads is not allowed to be taken out of the church. I promised Mari to be quiet at that moment and pray at my house. I had an appropriate day off.

When the clock approached eleven in the morning that day, I sat down next to the table and quieted down, took the Bible to the table and began to pray the Our Father prayer. I prayed for that without ceasing, because I didn't know what else I would have prayed for.

An hour passed and I felt strange, something was wrong.

– This didn't go as it should, I thought.

Mari called me a few hours later.

– What, how did it go, tell me everything, I asked fiercely, barely giving Mari a chance to speak.
– At first it felt good when the priest started reading from that book, Mari said.
– What book was that?
– It said Exorcism on the cover, Mari said.
– Really? I wondered. I was amazed, so that's what is really being done, I thought.
– Yes, but there should have been someone else reading too. You should have been present there. The priest didn't like that I came alone, Mari

explained.
– Oh no!! I exclaimed. – I felt like everything was not going as it should.
– It didn't work, Mari said. – Those spirits came back when I left the church.

I promised to pray for Mari again in the evening.

– Whatever, everything is fine, Mari said in pain.

Mari couldn't call the spirits demons, because they reacted to it. Mari always faced stronger attacks when she tried to talk about them. They had filled Mari's head, mind and body. The demons controlled her and didn't want anyone to save her. Mari was whispering on the phone and suddenly changed the subject. The demons were listening and tormented her as soon as she tried to mention them to me. I was a red garment to them.

The next day, Mari called. She felt how those spirits were even more aggressive than before.

– I couldn't sleep at all. They come and go all the time through me, Mari wailed.
– They didn't like what I did. Now they are really powerful and come with great force. It was hard for me to understand Mari's words, she seemed to be in pain. I felt despair for Mari, but I said:

– Mari you can't give up now, you'll get through this!

Mari said that the spirits come and go through her, especially at night, and if she tries to stop them, they are even stronger. Then she lets them through. Mari also said that they suck all the strength out of her.

– I don't think I can take it anymore, Ella, Mari moaned.
– Pray Mari, pray to Jesus in your life, I said excitedly. I didn't want to end the call, because I was afraid of what Mari would do.
– Let's call tomorrow, shall we? I asked.
– Let's do that, Mari answered in a slightly more cheerful voice.

– How do you feel today, Mari? I asked when I called Mari the next day.
– Better, maybe this will clear up, Mari said. We talked about everything usual, and I asked Mari to call if there was a need to talk.
– I'm praying for you, Mari, I said at the end.

I started to get tired of helping and felt bad about it. However, I prayed daily for Mari.

I let the time pass and focused on my own things so that I wouldn't be completely exhausted. Almost half a year had already passed with this helping. It made me tired, and I felt inadequate.

When I next talked with Mari on the phone, she said that she had asked Jesus and when she tried to follow Jesus' teachings, the spirits were even stronger and fought back, sucking her energy and taking over her head and whole body. But Mari promised to pray.

Time passed, and Mari informed me that she was starting psychotherapy. I was happy for Mari, she definitely needed it, but I was still worried that it wouldn't solve the problem she was having with the evil spirit world.

When Mari then talked about the psychotherapist, it turned out that she was a spiritualist. That combination was an abomination to me, but Mari felt good about it. I decided not to interfere too much in Mari's life, because I couldn't change anything.

I decided to let time pass and see if Mari could still get help from that professional helper.

Then Mari called and said that she feels that things are starting to go in the right direction.

– Sometimes I feel really bad, Mari said. – But we are on the right track, she continued. – The connection with God and Jesus is getting stronger all the time, and they are present almost constantly. They are also trying to give me power so I can fight evil. Jesus gives instructions and I follow, Mari said. – Evil fights hard and sucks energy from me and takes over my body, my head and everything. I pray this will be over soon, Mari continued.

I listened quietly. I wondered if God and Jesus really were with her, or did she said that to please me, or was that again caused by some evil spirits. According to her, Jesus had appeared to Mari, but then it wasn't Jesus after all, but the devil. And I knew that the devil had forbidden Mary to tell me anything at all. It was also difficult for Mari to speak out about evil, because then it always intensified.

– Be strong in your faith Mari, I'm praying for you too. And know that light overcomes darkness, I replied to Mari.

I felt sorry for Mari's situation, you couldn't believe it was true, but it was true. Where I had been on my way to... I was in the lucky position that I had gotten away from where Mari had "drowned" at the last moment.

Several months passed again and then I decided to message Mari to ask what was going on. She replied that there was something better and that she had been on a spiritual course dealing with Karma.

Mari wrote that she wanted this trainer's perspective on the matter and that her own thoughts would become clearer. She added that God and Jesus are getting stronger in her life every moment.

I let out a deep sigh. I was really disappointed because I knew that God and not Jesus would lead anyone to a spiritual course to find out Karma. I felt I had to give up and leave this matter in bigger hands. I wanted to help a friend, but now I am helping by praying for her.

This case of Mari made me exhausted, and I felt the first symptoms of depression as well. I did not understand at that time that my faith cannot help others. I was not in a living faith, and at the time I didn't even know the meaning of that word. All I felt was failure and disappointment. All I thought at the time was that my faith was not strong enough to help a friend. I didn't know how to proceed.

Later, when I've thought about it, I've noticed a deeply rooted element of a New Age, where I myself am the enabler of everything. I can, I believe, I heal, I save.

I had encountered faith, but I was still very deep in the grips of New Age, in the deep embrace of me and selfishness.

How could a person be able to save anyone else. Only God saves.

Of course you can help. And you can pray for your neighbor and with your neighbor. You can tell people about faith and thus lead them to encounter saving faith, but at that time my starting point was still far from that. I just didn't see it yet. How misguided I was when I thought I was doing good.

But God showed me even later that I was still very lost.

At that time, I was still struggling, but it's no wonder, because I was taking the first steps of my faith.

TWENTY-ONE

I had given up doing energy healing therapies almost entirely. I refused to take on new customers.

However, I decided to continue energy therapies in my own way for a few clients. I told them that this is different now. I thought that evil would not intervene if I always prayed for the clients and for myself before the therapy.

I really thought I could go on like that, but it started to feel more and more wrong each time.

In the end, I just couldn't anymore and was in pain. The energy healing therapies were not according to God's will, He revealed it to me.

I had to stop doing energy therapies altogether. They had been a source of income for me, but it meant nothing in the face of this larger cause.

I continued to do massages alongside my day job, without anything related to New Age.

I felt that God gave me a second chance and gradually began to remove things from my life that were not in accordance with God's will.
I sent an SMS to few remaining energy therapy clients. I explained in the message that I don't do these therapies anymore, I can't, and I don't want to. I told them that I believe in God and energy healing is not God's will.

These clients were very disappointed and angry. I expected it. I felt great relief when I got those messages sent and even greater relief knowing that I would never have to do energy therapies again.

About six months passed and I was contacted by a woman of faith. She had had my massage some years ago and remembered her as a very warm person.

She was talking about Jesus and salvation to me years ago. I also remember her mentioning that she was worried about certain therapies I was doing. She also asked me about yoga, but I told her I quit it a couple of years ago.

I was excited about her arrival, I wanted to tell her that I had found Jesus and let go of the of New Age.

When she heard this, she hugged me and said she and her husband prayed for me.

She had a massage three times and she gave me a lot. She led me to study different churches, because a believer needs a home for her faith.
I also told her that my family, and no one else knows about my coming to faith yet. The big problem for me was that the rest of my family doesn't believe in God and my own child professed to be an atheist.

– Ella, you can always pray for them so that God will glorify their way in Jesus Christ, said the woman, who had been brought into my life at this very moment as a gift from heaven. And so I started praying for it every day.

At the last massage, the woman said she wanted to pray for me. I clasped my hands, closed my eyes, and bowed my head. As she prayed in that therapy room for me and my family, tears came to my eyes. In my mind, I thanked God for him.

As she was leaving, she handed me another copy of the New Testament to read. My heart filled with joy, and I thanked her.

When I went to the store after that incident, I met my old colleague Kaija, whom I had last seen years ago.

When I was in my thirties, Kaija and I worked in the same office and talked a lot about our personal matters to each other.
I knew Kaija belonged to a sect, but we never talked about it.
It would have been quite uncomfortable for me to talk about it at the time, and I did not know how to deal with it.
    At that time, Kaija's sister was seriously ill and one day Kaija asked me if I would pray with her for her sister. I went completely locked up and couldn't find the right words. – I don't know, I don't..., I muttered.
– It's okay, Kaija said and smiled. That smile was forced.
– I don't mean..., I tried to fix it, but it only added to the pain of the situation.
    Kaija went to the ladies' room and I'm quite sure she cried there. I berated myself for saying that.
    I had been cruel. I always regretted that moment, but it was never talked about. Kaija's sister died a few months after that.

Now, just that evening, Kaija walked up to me, and I stopped her. She was cheerful, as she always

did when we rarely met. I was also extremely glad
to see her this very evening.

Kaija barely had time to ask how I was doing
when the speech started to pop out of my mouth.

– I'm fine Kaija, very especially fine, I said with a
smile. I have found God, Jesus Christ.

– Oh, Kaija said, putting her hand over her open
mouth. I could see tears coming up in her eyes.

– Lovely Ella, she said and hugged me tightly.

– Kaija, I want to apologize to you for doing
something, or rather for not doing it. I remember
you asking me to pray for your sister, and I didn't.
I'm so sorry for that, I said solemnly, meaning
every word from the heart.

More tears welled up in Kaija's eyes and she
nodded. She hugged me again and I was relieved
that I was able to say that to Kaija.

The rest of the way to the store, I smiled at
everyone I saw and wanted to hug each and every
one of them.

At home I cautiously told my husband about my
faith before going to bed. During the years of New
Age, he hadn't interfered with my "nonsense," as
he called it. – You can do that banter if you want,
if I don't have to participate, he always said.

I was nervous to bring it up, but then I was
encouraged.

– I'm in faith, I'm no longer spiritualist, I told him.
– What do you mean? He asked, his brows
furrowed.
– I believe in God, I've always believed, I replied.
– Have you become a believer? My husband
replied, looking disgusted. I became really sad
about that attitude of my husband.
– I've always believed in God. Isn't it better now to
believe in Jesus Christ than in unicorns and
witches? I asked ironically. – Oh yes, he replied,
clearly left with serious thoughts. I quickly
changed the subject, but it bothered me very much.

Then, as usual, when I went to bed before my
husband, I cried my eyes out of my head when I
got into the bedroom.
– What will happen to my marriage now? I
mourned in my mind. I have always prayed in the
evenings for my family and relatives, and for
others if I felt someone might need it. Now I
prayed to God that my husband could accept me
and my faith.

The next day I spoke to my son about it. I started
by apologizing for having done energy therapy for
him as a child and talking about New Age. At first,
he seemed to whine about it, but he was sensitive
to listening when I said that it was very important
to me.
– I'm sorry to have misled you as a child when I

talked to you about energies and New Age. I truly believed that they were in accordance with God's will, I said.

The boy listened.

– Do you remember when you were scared at night as a pre-teen and came to bed next to me? I asked.

– I remember because I felt like there was someone here in our house. I felt that way not so long ago, I wake up at night with the feeling that someone is looking at me, he astonished me with his speech.

– It's because I've been in contact with the spirit world. Forgive me, I said swallowing tears.

– Yup, he said.

– You can always ask Jesus to protect you, I said.

– Well, no, he protested.

– Really, give it a try, you can get a better night's sleep.

– I see, he muttered.

When I went to bed again, I cried. I felt deeply guilty about my son's depression, which had started few years ago and taken him into really dark waters. Part of it was probably due to his father's abuse and abandonment, but I had brought demons into his life through my own choices. I prayed for God's forgiveness and for my son to survive all this.

After a couple of days, my son told me quite
sharply that he does not believe in God at all, and
that is a great fairy tale for him. That hurt me hard!
However, I did not make any comment.

My son has received proper therapy and is
currently feeling better. He no longer denies when
I tell him about God and Jesus.
   My husband also said the other day that he
believes that Jesus existed, and he was guessing
there is a higher power out there as well. That
meant a lot to me. I thank God for that, I know my
prayers have been heard.

T W E N T Y - T W O

After coming to faith, I also met Saara, who had been in faith for ten years.

I had met her for the first time a couple of years ago at a friend's candle party. At that time, after the party, we stayed next to our cars to chat, because she wanted to say something to me.

I had mentioned something about being in New Age and she picked up on it. She told me about the Bible and the word of God. She also told how she had prayed for her energy healer friend when she wanted to accept Jesus in her life.

The story intrigued me at the time but didn't feel timely.

Now that we met again, at my friend's party, I pulled Saara aside before going home and asked her about the news. After a few usual hearings, Saara started to talk about conspiracies almost in a whisper, and then she started talking about faith.

– This is all a scam, Saara began. – You can't trust anyone. There are many truths, Saara said.

I was stunned by Sara's speech, and it was hard for me to breathe. I couldn't get a word out of my mouth when Saara already continued:

– In every religion, there is some guy at the tip of a stick, how would Jesus be somehow different.

I was shocked and felt bad. I had thought about telling Sarah about my faith, but I was so tired that I couldn't do anything. I left. Sarah had turned away from Jesus and even worse, mocked Him, mocked God. I prayed for Sarah. I didn't see Sarah again.

TWENTY-THREE

I decided to rummage through my bookshelves to find all the books on New Age that I wanted to get rid of. And I found several of them. It saddened me that I hadn't realized how to dispose of them earlier. However, somewhere there was a need for a hard disposal frenzy, and there were heaps of things to burn. Books worth hundreds of euros were now burning to ashes in the fireplace.

I deleted all New Age material, articles and pictures from my computer and email. I also deleted pictures and texts from social media, but unfortunately, I noticed that not everything can be deleted. There was no way I wanted to be seen as a spiritualist or New Ageist anymore, it felt so bad. I also disposed of the pendulum, dream catchers and Buddha statues from my home. Some of those statues had been in my home for a couple of ten years, because I had brought them as souvenirs.

They found their way to garbage can; I didn't want idols in my home.

I threw away all the crystals I had used to protect, empower, ground, heal, give spiritual powers, etc. I didn't want or need any more magic items or amulets.

In faith in God, I am enough just as I am, everything else is useless and superstition.

Some people sleep with crystals under their pillow or buy pocket stones to be protected, "safe", to get energy, peace, etc. That's what I did too, but now it seemed pointless. It was connected to New Age, and I wanted to cut off absolutely every connection with that branch of occultism.

When Man becomes a child of God, nothing external is needed anymore. Everything about the New Age felt distorted; God had shown me that it was delusion.

New Age also includes burning dried white sage or incense in places where you want to cleanse negative energy. I used to do that myself. Now the sages and incense were allowed to leave. The New Age emphasizes the good and the fact that when you focus on the good, you will also get it. So that removal of negative energy is somehow contradictory, like many other things in the New Age.

In New Age, the devil is not recognized as being. According to it, some people are only in low or negative energies, and it feels heavy to be around them. That low energy can be caused by depression, anger, sadness, alcohol, etc. Negative emotions may therefore be avoided until the very end. Many try to be only in loving energies, no matter how low the mood is.

New Age healers often have trouble coping, many burn out, because repressed negative emotions may turn inward.

Many yo-yos with their emotions. They are afraid of losing face if the truth about the inability to cope is revealed. And since that loving energy of New Age is not caused by God, but by an opposing force, its magic does not last.
In my New Age years, I felt the presence of evil energy. At the time, though, I didn't know that absolutely everything I did came from the same source as the evil energy I felt. It was only in the "prettier package", but the truth finally came out, thank God.

My own opinion is that only evil denies itself. Evil has shown me so many faces that I can recognize it.

However, the devil is cunning, and is always trying to make an impact. That influence manifested itself and still manifests itself in my life, e.g. as a doubt. Here's one example: – Ella, are you absolutely sure now that it is the Holy Spirit who is speaking to you? I know what is behind those "bombings" and I will not let it discourage me. My faith is strong.

When I was doing energy healing therapies and messaging from spirit world, many people who attended my therapies called me an angel. They thought I was an earthly angel. I took it as a compliment, but I never felt like I was any angel. Sure, I was kind at heart, but I often felt anger and resentment inside me. I was never unkind to anyone, but that anger came when I was alone. Something in me was criticizing, nagging and invalidating myself and my relationship with others. Sometimes others too.

I couldn't admit that I was in "negative energies" at the time, they didn't exist. Well, in New Age, there seems to be another explanation for that, that I had been around a negatively charged person and that person's energy had entered my own energy field and I needed aura cleansing or energy therapy.

That same uncomfortable feeling made me extremely competitive – I wanted to be the best. I have been adopted one of Maiju's teachings. To be the best, or second best, as she said, because she was the best.

I was competitive even before I became New Ageist, spirituality only seemed to feed my feeling of inadequacy, which manifested itself as fierce competitiveness. I tried to hide that feeling and I succeeded very well. A spiritualist is simply only feeling huge love for oneself and others. Rubbish, I say to that now.

Spirituality (New Ageists prefer to call themselves "spiritual" rather than New Ageists) is big business and there is competition in it, just like in other business activities. They steal ideas and are rude.

Some were even so arrogant that they copied everything word for word and advertised it as their own. I could never imagine such rude behavior in deeply spiritual people.

The flower of envy blossomed here and there and turned people against each other. And the same continues.

All that inappropriate behavior was masked with inauthentic love. It is true that there were and still are many loving people in those circles, unfortunately they are very often the targets of abuse by the more spiritually "advanced ones". Many people want to help others from their heart and then get lost on different roads in the delusion of New Age.

They don't see any danger or risk in being there because it feels so wonderful and full of love. They don't question it because it feels right. I fell into the same trap.

But I understand now that Satan appears as an angel of light, creates energies that feel wonderful and can create supernatural phenomena. And is quite a credible liar. Its lovingness is not true, but false.

It also made me believe that I could heal people with energies and Healing. And still, only God can heal. Man cannot take credit for it, or strive to take on God's tasks, that is not helping, but striving to be God.

That pursuit is straight from Satan. It can make things happened and even momentary healing, but nothing it promises lasts.

There are many tools of Satan and I immersed myself in New Age.
New Age is not from God, it IS from Satan. Satan wants a person completely, at any cost.
When I delved into the background of the New Age, I found that its roots go back to the theosophist Helena Blavatsky and Alice Bailey, who was familiar with her literature.

Their world of values was based on e.g. to the occult. Occultism is e.g. New Age, which Bailey was one of the first to write about.

The New Age and its various branches: energy healing, channeling, mediums, numerology, witchcraft, shamanism, spirit guides, angel therapies, aura cleansing, karma removal, Tarot cards, etc. are from the devil, Satan, who misleads and leads astray and ultimately to destruction. You may be reacting to this now, as I did years ago when I was first told that energy healing is from the devil.

I got really angry, because I thought I was right. I was horrified by the fact that a believer would tell me straight to my face that I was under the control of the devil. For me, who had discovered the truth about New Age and experienced all kinds of wonderful things and miracles, omens and signs. For me, who had found my own truth, and he was trying to shake it. My soul and heart flashed at that time; I was so full of "holy hatred" towards that person.

Now I've seen it myself. Now I believe. That man of faith was right, and I am grateful for his reaction and his words.
I was in the New Age for 15 years, I was there, – I know!

TWENTY-FOUR

After becoming in faith, that competitive spirit, anger and feeling of inadequacy disappeared. I realized that it was also an "alley run" caused by the devil.

Sure, I still get angry and resentful, but it only lasts for a while. Nowadays, I also pray for those who I considered to be my competitors.

Even as a small child, I often felt an immense sense of longing, for which there was no explanation. That longing has been with me all my life and I've looked for all kinds of reasons for it.

Renewal was one of my wanderings to find a reason to miss, but when I found Jesus, I finally knew what I had been missing.

Sometimes I wonder if I'm really in the faith when I haven't experienced any "charm", but it's not necessary. Those Gods words from a couple of years ago is still vividly in my mind. And God guides me daily. Every day I learn something new on my Christian path, which is just beginning.

I also suddenly noticed that I was no longer afraid of what I had been afraid of before. Unbelievable peace descended on me with faith, and I feel that no matter what happens, peace remains.

I became interested in various Christian films and Christian speakers. I stumbled across Derek Prince's YouTube videos. His interpretations of the Bible were very meaningful to me.

Prince talks a lot about the devil and curses, and I subscribe to many of his teachings. We may unconsciously curse our children and ourselves. Those curses may also be from generations ago and still affect our own lives today.

Prince's teachings really spoke to me based on everything I experienced. I bought Prince's books and, in his books, he talks about numerous cases where he has released curses from people and prayed for them.

I began to pray for deliverance for myself and my family from all the evil that I had caused myself or that could be something negative caused by my parents and their parents.

TWENTY-FIVE

The devil is more cunning than us, we can't handle
him in cunning.
Neither can we control it, nor the forces it controls.
When we do or attend various energy therapies,
angel therapies, messaging, channeling, etc., we
open the door to the devil.
We can't really handle the devil anywhere, even
if we think so. Only God, Jesus Christ, the Holy
Spirit can do that. We should ask Him for help in
the fight against evil. He is the only light and truth.
The devil pretends to be deceased loved ones,
angels, spirit guides, etc. It may seem wonderful at
first, after all, the master liar Satan himself is
behind it all. He is brilliant in his role. No one who
wants good for other people would consciously
follow Satan, that's why he must pretend to be
something else that makes people possessed. He

makes them believe in his liars and make people always want more.

Almost everyone who has had energy therapies or healing wants more of it. Those who have visited clairvoyant will almost certainly go again.

Those who participated in the medium's message transmissions usually don't go there once. The devil entices, he is a master at that too.

Angel therapy that feels gentle may seem so wonderful that it wouldn't even occur to you that there is something evil behind it.

The persons doing these therapies themselves are often very sympathetic and considerate. They don't understand, and on the other hand they don't want to understand, or they don't believe that there could be anything wrong with these wonderful "energies". These therapies will open the door for spirits to influence both those ones giving these treatments and the client.

In the same way, people apply for New Age courses to seek their own strength, spiritual development, etc. again and again. There is no end to spiritual development, you are never ready. The devil knows how important we are to ourselves, and that's why that own power appeals to us in a magical way.

We may think: – What could I be... but the human being has self-sufficient only up to a certain point.

God is the power we should trust, we ourselves are deficient. The path of one's own power leads astray, God's path leads to truth.
You will understand this when you are saved by God. After all, we don't refuse someone trying to save us even when we are to be drowning in water. We don't say, "no thanks, I will be saved by my own power".

There are many different New Age courses, and several of them are quite expensive. These courses are promising for example expanding consciousness, raising vibration levels, empowerment, finding the inner child, spiritual growth, change in life direction, etc.

Ego may be boosted by the image of being a Goddess. There are numerous courses for such training as well.

Endless abundance and money are also promised by many New Age influencers in their online courses.

I once almost signed up for a free Abundance and Money Manifestation course, which in the end would have cost €4,000.

I stated that the author of that course had really manifested money for herself at the expense of others. Manifestation is a term in New Age that says you can get anything if you believe enough to get it. If you don't get it, you haven't believed enough, and you obviously need a new course to strengthen your faith. There are unfortunately many of these financiers of the unsuspecting in the New Age.

T W E N T Y – S I X

After coming to faith, I started acquiring Christian literature and joined ex–New Age and faith groups on social media. Those groups were a lot of help, because peer support is exactly what people who break away from the New Age need.

The years-long connection with New Age people was strong for me. Almost my entire circle of friends consisted of those people. Perhaps the most annoying thing was that my friends rejected me when they heard about my faith. It was easier to find fellow sisters with the same experience, even if only on social media.

I was looking for a spiritual home for my faith; I waded through the Internet, presentations of different trends and websites.

I noticed to my great disappointment that the church I had belonged to all my life began to approach the New Age with real action. One priest even said that he uses Tarot cards and called them the cards of Mercy.

I also noticed that many representatives of the church were very sympathetic to the New Age from which I had just been saved.

I decided to give myself time and pray to God to show me my home of faith. And I have time, I don't need to develop myself anymore and strive for higher frequencies, vibrations or dimensions and jump in expensive New Age trainings.

Faith in Jesus Christ is free of charge and gives much more than anything else, it gives peace and grace.

I started reading the New Testament of the Bible every evening. I had my grandmother's old Bible on my bookshelf, but I felt it was important to have my very own, so I ordered one. I experienced great joy when the package arrived in the mail, and I was able to open my own Bible.

During breakfast and jogging, I listen to the Old Testament as a podcast. The texts of the Bible do not fully open to me yet, but I know that reading the Word brings me closer to God. I don't have to understand everything yet, the effect of the Word is guaranteed, because it is from God. Many verses of the Bible can only be opened in later readings. However, I immediately found many verses that I wanted to underline. I've thought about reading the Bible many times over the years, but it's always stuck. I haven't been able to do it or something else, usually a book with a New Age has been more interesting. Now it was different. I had become thirsty for the Bible and God.

In the evening, after the Bible chapter, I thank God and pray for my family and all my loved ones. I also pray for those who have asked me for help. I also pray for all the people mentioned in this book. Their names and some events have been changed to keep their identities secret.

This book is my experience of it, of what happened to me. Everything that happened has brought me to where I am now: In faith in Jesus Christ. I have found the truth, there is only one truth.

My advice to you, dear reader: Ask Jesus into your heart and receive peace in the face of everything.
   When we humble ourselves and confess our sins, it will be heard. Then pray for access to God in Jesus Christ and the Holy Spirit.
It enables connection with God.
Only God can save us.

If this still doesn't seem relevant, you can come back to it at any time. God is not in a hurry, and He always welcomes you with open arms.

Blessings to you reader,
with love,
Ella

REFERENCES

Internet:

https://www.bbc.co.uk/religion/religions/spiritualis
m/ataglance/glance.shtml

https://www.lucistrust.org/

https://en.wikipedia.org/wiki/Alice_Bailey

https://fi.wikipedia.org/wiki/H._P._Blavatsky

https://www.kirkkojakaupunki.fi/–/–jos–tarot–
sana–tuntuu–pahalta–naita–voisi–nimittaa–armon–
korteiksi–pappi–henri–jarvinen–kayttaa–tarot–
kortteja–itsetuntemuksen–lisaamiseen

Literature:

Holy Bible (1938), the eleventh, Finnish translation put into practice by the general Church Council held in 1933. Turku: Suomen Pipliaseura.

Prince, Derek (2018): Blessing or Curse – You Can Choose. Helsinki: Lighthouse Network Ltd Oy/ TV7 Kustannus